Twayne's United States Authors Series

Sylvia E. Bowman, *Editor*

INDIANA UNIVERSITY

Christopher Morley

TUSAS 278

Christopher Morley

CHRISTOPHER MORLEY

By MARK I. WALLACH and
JON BRACKER

TWAYNE PUBLISHERS
A DIVISION OF G. K. HALL & CO., BOSTON

Library of Congress Cataloging in Publication Data

Wallach, Mark I
   Christopher Morley.

   (Twayne's United States authors series ; TUSAS 278)
   Bibliography: p. 133 - 39.
   Includes index.
   1. Morley, Christopher Darlington, 1890-1957.
I. Bracker, Jonathan, 1936-   joint author.
PS3525.071Z95   818'.5'209   76-17922
ISBN 0-8057-7178-6

MANUFACTURED IN THE UNITED STATES OF AMERICA

Contents

About the Authors

Mark I. Wallach first became interested in Christopher Morley's works while an undergraduate in the College of Social Studies of Wesleyan University, Middletown, Connecticut, where he received his Bachelor of Arts Degree in 1971.

He graduated from Harvard Law School, Cambridge, Massachusetts, in 1974, and was admitted to the Bar of the State of Ohio later that year. Following law school he served as law clerk to Chief Judge Frank J. Battisti of the United States District Court, Northern District of Ohio, and is presently associated with the Cleveland, Ohio, law firm of Baker, Hostetler & Patterson.

His earliest publication was a short study, "The Essays and Columns of Christopher Morley," which appeared in *The Markham Review* in February, 1972. A major legal analysis entitled "Whose Intent? A Study of Preemption by Administrative Agencies: State Regulation of Cable Television," was published in the Winter, 1975, issue of the *Case Western Reserve Law Review*.

Jon Bracker is the editor of *Bright Cages, the Selected Poems of Christopher Morley*, published in 1965, and is the cataloguer of the Morley Estate papers at the Humanities Research Center of the University of Texas.

Specializing in creative writing and poetry, he has taught English at Amarillo College, Midwestern University, Slippery Rock State College, Indiana State University, as Poet-in-Residence in the Muncie, Indiana, public schools, and aboard the U.S.S. *Kitty Hawk*, under the P.A.C.E. program administered for the U.S. Navy by Chapman College.

His poems have appeared in a number of magazines and anthologies, and in two chapbooks, *Constellations of Clover*, published in 1973, and *California and Other Poems*, issued in 1976. A recent manuscript of verse, "World Enough," is as yet unpublished.

Preface

Christopher Morley is a puzzle: one of the best-known and most in-fluential figures of his time in the world of American belles lettres, he is today virtually unknown to younger readers. Simultaneously a scholar, a popularizer, a publicist, a businessman, and a fine writer of many types of literature, Morley has been forgotten in school curricula and has vanished from the writings of American critics.

Why has Morley become so nearly unknown in so short a time? Do the details of his life hold the key to his successful and wide-ranging career and to his subsequent eclipse? How did he manage to in-tegrate so many forms of literary activity into one lifetime — and with what effects? This book attempts to answer these questions by painting a portrait of Christopher Morley, through his life and writings, as a professional literary man with a unique approach to literature and to the culture surrounding it.

Morley's fascination with writing and writers is crucial to this con-ception of his works and career since it was both a motivating and a unifying force in his life. One of the main contentions of this study, in fact, is that there is no real disjunction between Morley's writings and the other aspects of his life and career. Chapters treating various aspects of Christopher Morley have been carved out largely on the basis of convenience and without any contention that the divisions thus created represent discrete portions of Morley's life and work.

A biographical sketch places Morley in chronological perspective, as well as introduces him to the reader in all of his many roles simultaneously. This chapter focuses on Morley's efforts as a publicist, a figure who devoted large amounts of his time and talent to promoting the work of other writers. Besides representing a major area of Christopher Morley's career, this section illustrates the con-tinuity between his activities as a writer and his non-writing roles.

Each of the following three chapters attempts to deal with one of Christopher Morley's other major career roles. The first of these explores Morley's columns and other essays; since most of his published volumes of essays are drawn from his newspaper and magazine columns, it would be difficult to treat these topics separately. Morley's essays were perhaps the most uniformly well received of all his writing, and they appeared in virtually all of the leading journals of his day, despite the fact that most were composed to meet daily or weekly deadlines.

Christopher Morley is best remembered today as a novelist, and won his greatest fame in that field. With few exceptions, however, his novels were automatically restricted in readership by Morley's predominant interest in the relationship between literature and life, which expressed itself clearly in most of his novels. Morley, however, liked to think of himself primarily as a poet, although his poetry had less commercial success than much of his other work. While most of his poetry was quite traditional, Morley created a new form that he called "Translations from the Chinese," which proved to be an excellent medium for his temperament and thoughts. The chapter dealing with his poetry emphasizes Morley's deep involvement with literary questions as well as with other poets.

The concluding chapter attempts to combine Morley's own appraisal of what literature is about, and where his own place in its world was located, with the evidence drawn from Morley's career and writings. Relying partly on several lectures that Morley gave to college audiences, the conclusion tries to integrate Morley's many roles as writer and literary personage to establish an accurate picture of his career, as well as to place him in the perspective of the American literary scene in the first half of the twentieth century.

MARK I. WALLACH
JON BRACKER

Acknowledgments

The authors acknowledge their indebtedness to the following publishers and individuals for permission to quote from a variety of sources:

J. B. Lippincott Company for the following: "The Cigarette Stub," "Bivalves," "Only Word of Mouth," and "The Palimpsest," from *Poems and Translations from the Chinese* by Christopher Morley. Copyright 1929 by Doubleday, Doran and Company. Copyright © renewed 1957 by Christopher Morley. Reprinted by permission of J. B. Lippincott Company. "At the Mermaid Cafeteria," "Charles and Mary," "A Grub Street Recessional," "Of a Child That Had Fever," and 8 lines from "To a Very Young Gentleman," from *Chimneysmoke* by Christopher Morley. Copyright 1921, renewed 1949 by Christopher Morley. Reprinted by permission of J. B. Lippincott Company. "Pragmatism" and "The Epigram," from *Parson's Pleasure* by Christopher Morley. Copyright 1923, renewed 1951 by Christopher Morley. Reprinted by permission of J. B. Lippincott Company. "Stop-Short" from *Mandarin in Manhattan* by Christopher Morley. Copyright 1933 by Christopher Morley. Copyright © renewed 1961 by Mrs. Helen F. Morley. Reprinted by permission of J. B. Lippincott Company. Excerpts from *Parnassus on Wheels* by Christopher Morley. Copyright 1917, 1945 by Christopher Morley. Reprinted by permission of J. B. Lippincott Company. Excerpts from *The Haunted Bookshop* by Christopher Morley. Copyright 1919, 1923, 1946, 1951 by Christopher Morley. Reprinted by permission of J. B. Lippincott Company. Excerpts from *Where the Blue Begins* by Christopher Morley. Copyright 1922, 1927 by Doubleday, Page & Co. Copyright renewed 1950 by Christopher Morley. Reprinted by permission of J. B. Lippincott Company. Excerpts from *Thunder on the Left* by Christopher Morley. Copyright 1925, renewed 1953 by

Chronology

1890   Christopher Darlington Morley born May 5, the eldest of three sons, to Lilian Bird Morley and Frank Morley in Haverford, Pennsylvania.

1900   The family moves to Baltimore, where Frank Morley, a noted mathematician, teaches at Johns Hopkins University.

1906 - Attends Haverford College; edits school literary magazine
1910   and is elected to Phi Beta Kappa.

1910 - Studies modern history at New College, Oxford, as a Rhodes
1913   scholar.

1912   Publishes in England *The Eighth Sin,* his first volume of poetry.

1913 - Works for Doubleday, Page and Company at Garden City,
1917   New York, learning every aspect of the book trade.

1914   Marries Helen Booth Fairchild; they later have four children, Christopher, Jr., Louise, Helen, and Blythe.

1917 - Lives in Philadelphia, first as an editor of the *Ladies' Home*
1920   *Journal,* then as columnist for the *Philadelphia Evening Public Ledger.*

1918   Publishes *Shandygaff,* the first of thirteen collections of essays.

1920   Begins life-long residence at "The Birches," Roslyn, Long Island, New York.

1920 - Conducts "The Bowling Green" column in the *New York*
1923   *Evening Post.*

1922   Publishes *Where the Blue Begins;* edits *Modern Essays,* a popular anthology for schools.

1924 - Acts as contributing editor of *The Saturday Review of Liter-*
1941   *ature,* conducting "The Bowling Green" column for fourteen years, and the "Trade Winds" department for fifteen.

1925   Publishes *Thunder on the Left.*

1926 -   Serves as judge of the Book-of-the-Month Club.
1954

1927   Doubleday publishes twelve-volume *Haverford Collected Edition* of Morley's works.

1928 -   Presents popular series of old melodramas at two theaters in
1930   Hoboken, New Jersey.

1931   Publishes the autobiographical *John Mistletoe;* lectures at the University of Pennsylvania (published as *Ex Libris Carissimis*).

1932   Publishes *Human Being.*

1933   Founds the Baker Street Irregulars.

1937   Edits the eleventh edition of Bartlett's *Familiar Quotations* with the assistance of Louella Everett.

1938   Publishes *History of an Autumn,* long essay on events at Munich.

1939   Publishes *Kitty Foyle,* his best-selling novel.

1942   Publishes *Thorofare.*

1948   Publishes revised twelfth edition of Bartlett's *Familiar Quotations.*

1949   Publishes *The Man Who Made Friends With Himself,* his last novel.

1951   Suffers the first of three incapacitating strokes.

1955   Publishes *Gentlemen's Relish,* his last volume of poems.

1957   Morley dies, March 28.

CHAPTER 1

A Biographical Sketch of
Christopher Morley

I The Factual Framework

AT the age of forty Christopher Darlington Morley decided to write a novel about himself, to record and thereby close the chapter of his life entitled "Youth." The book — *John Mistletoe* — consists of a collection of essays, anecdotes, stories, some verse, and numbers of newspaper columns, all arranged to approximate narrative form. This variegated collection is a particularly appropriate portrait of Morley's career, both as it stood before the composition of *John Mistletoe* in 1930, and as it was to proceed for the next twenty-five years. Including virtually all forms of literary activity, *John Mistletoe* reveals the breadth of Christopher Morley's involvement in the literary world but, at the same time, presents examples of the depth of his thought.

Christopher Morley was born in Haverford, Pennsylvania, on May 5, 1890. Both of his parents were English by birth; his father, Frank Morley, was a distinguished mathematician who had come to Haverford College three years before his son's birth. Morley's mother was a musician and poet whose father had worked for Chapman and Hall, a famous English publishing house; this connection to the "greats" of English literature was one that Christopher Morley loved to speculate about and discuss.

Morley's first ten years were spent in Haverford, a suburb of Philadelphia, which in the 1890's was an unspoiled area of wide lawns and majestic trees; in *John Mistletoe*, Morley recalled this environment as the happiest of his life, one that was ideal for a growing boy. Although his family moved to Baltimore in 1900 to enable Professor Morley to take a chair in pure mathematics at Johns Hopkins University, Christopher returned to Haverford six years later as an undergraduate. He graduated as valedictorian of his class,

13

was awarded a membership in Phi Beta Kappa, and won a Rhodes scholarship. During his undergraduate years Morley contributed extensively to and helped edit *The Haverfordian*, the student literary magazine; in 1925, some of these essays, stories, and poems were published by Haverford under the title, *Hostages To Fortune*. One of his lifelong literary passions appears in this small volume, an essay on Robert Louis Stevenson exhibiting the gently publicizing vein that Morley was to develop into a mainstay of his writing.

Morley's Rhodes scholarship gave him three years at New College, Oxford, where he studied history and where he also published his first book, the small volume of poems *The Eighth Sin*. Appearing under the imprint of B. H. Blackwell, the Oxford bookseller, *The Eighth Sin* was dedicated to Helen Booth Fairchild, an American girl Morley met while in England. The title was drawn from a passage in the letters of John Keats: "There is no greater sin after the seven deadly than to flatter oneself into an idea of being a great Poet." Morley's collection created no literary ripples, and he reprinted only one of its poems in later volumes; nevertheless, *The Eighth Sin* is today prized a a rare collector's item that brings more than six hundred dollars a copy in the rare book market.[1] Some years later, Oxford was to serve as the locale for an early novel of Morley's entitled *Kathleen*, one of his most genuinely undistinguished works.

When Christopher Morley returned to America in 1913, he went immediately to Doubleday, Page and Company to ask for a job in the publishing industry. There he confronted F. N. Doubleday ("Effendi," as Morley invariably referred to him, adopting Rudyard Kipling's nickname for Doubleday) in a much publicized incident which Doubleday recounted some years later:

He told me of his career from boyhood to very early manhood, and he was delightfully young with an enthusiasm which was very appealing . . . he thought, as others have, that the most delightful way to earn his living would be to become part of a publishing house, and Garden City, he added, looked good to him. . . .

To get a breathing space I asked him if he had any plans along book lines on which a modest publisher could make a few stray dollars. This was indeed an opening. Morley immediately dove into a deep pocket and produced a large number of papers on which were worked out books and plans for series of books in vast array — names of authors in ample numbers who have beyond the shadow of doubt the divine fire, and I confess I found his enthusiasm most contagious. . . . He had it in his mind evidently that he had come to a publisher to talk books, not finance. . . .

. . . Finally I said to him, 'You would have to be about ten men to successfully carry out all these plans; now if you had your choice of any job in the place what would you choose?' Without a second's hesitation he said, 'Yours.'[2]

Morley was given a job, albeit not Effendi's own. During his tenure with Doubleday Morley married Helen Fairchild, the girl he had met in England, who was to be the author of many children's books. They began housekeeping on Long Island, with Morley working as a Doubleday publicist, reading and judging manuscripts, as well as dealing directly with booksellers to encourage the sales of Doubleday authors.

Although the Morley-Doubleday collaboration continued for many years, with Doubleday publishing the bulk of Morley's works, Christopher Morley and his wife moved to Wyncote, Pennsylvania, in 1917, where he took a job as editor of the *Ladies' Home Journal,* and later moved to the *Philadelphia Evening Public Ledger* which printed his first newspaper column. While in Philadelphia, Morley wrote his first novel, *Parnassus on Wheels;* he also published a collection of his early columns as *Travels in Philadelphia,* describing his pedestrian meanderings through that city.

When the Morleys returned to New York in 1920, they settled in Roslyn, Long Island, in the house that was to be their lifelong home. From 1920 until his death in 1957 Morley did much of his writing at home, either in his study in the house or in "The Knothole," a one-room log cabin he had built in 1935 in back of his house. Not until 1939 did he spend much time writing in New York; at that time he rented an office on Forty-seventh Street that he called "Sciatica" because the elevator-less building aggravated his susceptibility to that disease. From 1920 to 1923 Morley wrote the column "The Bowling Green" for the *New York Evening Post;* he patterned it after Don Marquis's "The Sun Dial." Both columns contained frequent light essays by their authors, but they also included samples of the works of new writers and the news of recent literary developments. "The Bowling Green" continued through Morley's move to the new *Saturday Review of Literature* in 1924 and until his retirement from that publication in 1941. In addition to "The Bowling Green," Morley's duties on *The Saturday Review* included a contributing editorship and another column (later continued under Cleveland Amory's authorship) called "Trade Winds."

Following the considerable success of *Parnassus On Wheels,* which described the adventures of a travelling bookseller, Morley began writing at a heavy pace. *Songs for a Little House*, published in 1917, was Morley's first important volume of poetry; it was largely in the domestic vein he continued for several years. *Shandygaff*, Morley's first volume of essays, appeared in 1918; the material was taken mostly from his newspaper columns, thereby setting a precedent that was to continue through virtually all of his eighteen collections of essays. Morley's poetry filled eighteen complete volumes, but some of his poems also appeared in books comprised chiefly of essays and short stories.[3] A number of one-act plays appeared during the 1920's and 1930's, besides several dramatizations of his novels and a full-length adaptation of *Troilus and Cressida* called *The Trojan Horse*. During the 1920's Morley also published several volumes of short stories.

When Christopher Morley followed *Parnassus* with a sequel, *The Haunted Bookshop*, in 1919, many critics felt that he was taking excessive measures to ingratiate himself with the bookselling industry; however, his preoccupation with books and the culture surrounding their publication and sale continued long after his career ceased to depend upon the special good-will of book merchants. *Human Being*, published in 1932, narrated the life of a travelling salesman who worked for a publishing house; a literary agent is the hero of *The Man Who Made Friends With Himself*, Morley's last novel (1949).

II   *Facets of Morley's Career*

Christopher Morley's career, however, included far more than the usual activities of a writer; for he penetrated virtually all enclaves of American literary culture. He became, in 1926, one of the original five members of the editorial board of the Book-of-the-Month Club, a group that contained such figures as Henry Seidel Canby, who was also Morley's associate on *The Saturday Review*, William Allen White, and Heywood Broun.[4] Morley's work for the club absorbed progressively larger portions of his time throughout the 1930's and 1940's; it was one of the last activities that Morley surrendered after his health began to fail in the early 1950's. He not only wrote hundreds of book reviews for the Book-of-the-Month Club News, but he also read and screened new manuscripts. Another activity that occasionally brought Morley into New York City was his infrequent appearance on the radio program "Information Please."

On numerous occasions Morley assumed the role of lecturer, usually speaking about some aspect of literature that fascinated him.

In 1930 Dr. A. S. W. Rosenbach, a noted book collector and bibliographer, founded a Fellowship in Bibliography at the University of Pennsylvania; and, after Christopher Morley was appointed in 1931 as the first Rosenbach Fellow, he delivered a series of talks in that capacity which were later published in a volume called *Ex Libris Carissimis*. Two years later Morley was invited to lecture at the University of Hawaii at Honolulu; his lectures there of March, 1933, were published as *Shakespeare and Hawaii*. Late in 1935 Morley spoke at Columbia University to commemorate the one-hundredth anniversary of Mark Twain's birth. Twain was also the topic of Morley's 1937 appearance at the University of Michigan, where he delivered the annual Hopwood address. The following year Christopher Morley was the William L. Honnold Foundation lecturer at Knox College, Illinois. During March and April of 1939 Morley gave a series of ten talks at Adelphi College, near his home in Roslyn Estates, Long Island, one of which was published as *Passivity Program* that year by *The Saturday Review of Literature* and by the Argus Book Shop of Chicago. R. Buckminster Fuller, Morley's friend, often accompanied him on the lecture tours of the 1930's; Fuller has commented that he would have found it difficult to support himself during that period without Morley's assistance and encouragement.[5]

One of Christopher Morley's most enduring enthusiasms was the fabled detective, Sherlock Holmes. Not only did Morley write the introduction to the only authoritative collected edition of Sherlock Holmes adventure stories — which is still in print — but he also helped found the Baker Street Irregulars. Established in 1934, the Baker Street Irregulars is an organization of true Holmes devotees, which publishes a journal of Sherlock Holmes scholarship to which Morley made frequent contributions.

After editing a brief but interesting anthology, *Ex Libris*, a collection of short selections about the art of reading which was sold at the First National Book Fair in New York City in 1936, Morley edited, with the assistance of Louella D. Everett, the first of two editions of Bartlett's *Familiar Quotations*, his most ambitious works as an anthologist. Morley was not unaware of the problem posed by the job: to preserve well-loved bad verse while also including lesser-known but better written phrases. "This is in no sense a collection of personal choices," Morley declared, but a compromise between "what readers want" and "what they ought to want." One of

Morley's first tasks was to fill some surprising gaps: Herman Melville, Emily Dickinson, and William Blake, none of whom had appeared in the previous Tenth Edition (1914), as well as Thomas De Quincey and William Hazlitt, who were found only in footnotes. To create space for his new additions, Morley omitted some excess William Wordsworth, some lesser Lord Byron, and lines by deservedly forgotten old favorites such as Thomas Kibble Hervey. The 1937 Eleventh Edition included not only Morley's special enthusiasms, but also the contemporary masters, Ernest Hemingway, E. E. Cummings, T. S. Eliot, and Ezra Pound; and few, if any, important writers were omitted. Particularly zestful are Morley's numerous footnotes, which give added information, anecdotes, and extensive cross-references.

Morley continued to oversee the quotations included in the Twelfth Edition in 1948. In that volume he allowed himself the luxury of introducing some of his own lines into the book — in addition to those in his regular entry — under the pseudonym Barclay Hall, a pen name he had used before in print. He also indulged in some private humor by ending the Miscellaneous and Translations Section with a Latin quotation, "Nunc scripsi totum; pro Christo da mihi potum," which was attributed to an unknown medieval monk. Few readers noticed the phrase, which translates as, "I've finished the job; for Christ's sake give me a drink."

His appointment as editor-in-chief of the *Bartlett's* revision led Morley to build himself a private writing room in the back yard of his Roslyn home; this small cabin, known as "The Knothole," became the origin for much of Morley's writing from that time until his death. The Knothole contained much of Morley's library, a large desk, a bunk for occasional naps, large windows, and inscriptions from friends who had visited him there. One, carved over Morley's bunk by Don Marquis, reads: "If you fall asleep while you're loafing, how are you going to know that you're loafing?"[6] After his death in 1957 a group of Morley's friends founded the Christopher Morley Knothole Association to preserve The Knothole "as a literary landmark."[7] This project was finally accomplished in 1966 when Nassau County opened Christopher Morley Park, the new home of The Knothole — now a Morley museum. The Knothole Association, meanwhile, has grown to international proportions in recent years; it acts both as a clearing-house for Morley scholarship and as a meeting-place for Morley enthusiasts.

Another of Morley's persistent interests was Walt Whitman, who, like Morley, was a Long Island resident. While Morley wrote numerous essays boosting Whitman's poetry, he felt even more strongly about his prose, which he believed had been neglected by American critics. In 1926 Morley wrote a lengthy introduction to an edition of Whitman's *Two Prefaces to Leaves of Grass*, in which he contended that "They are as important in American literature as the Gettysburg speech in American history."[8] For a 1940 volume of selections from *Leaves of Grass* Morley acted as editor, besides writing a critical preface. One of the six one-act plays that Morley included in his only volume of collected plays was a lengthy portrait of Whitman's last days entitled *Walt*. It is characteristic of Morley's whole career that he devoted numerous works over an extended period of time to the promotion of those works of another author that he felt to be neglected but valuable.

Christopher Morley's love for the theater extended far beyond the few plays he wrote himself. His first venture into theatrical production began in 1928 when he and Cleon Throckmorton took over the old Rialto and Lyric theaters in Hoboken, New Jersey; they had been popular in the 1860's as beer-gardens and as homes of melodrama. There Morley and Throckmorton began staging revivals of old melodramas, in styles faithful to the original productions. Although the project took some months to attract customers, clever advertising and the critical approval of Brooks Atkinson finally brought considerable success to the theaters as a kind of way-off-Broadway complex. Charles M. Barras's *The Black Crook* and Dion Boucicault's *After Dark* were two of the better-known revivals, while a dramatization of Morley's novel, *Pleased to Meet You*, with incidental music by Jerome Kern, ran for two weeks at the revitalized Rialto. In *Born in a Beer Garden*, one of the two books that Morley issued about the Hoboken experiment,[9] he estimated that "Between January and May 150,000 people packed themselves into that shabby little old playhouse."[10] Critic St. John Ervine wrote that the Hoboken revival pointed the way toward a decentralization of the New York theater,[11] and Ogden Nash was brought in by Morley and Throckmorton to write a publicity article.

Finally, however, in 1930, after a year of popular acclaim, the project collapsed with dwindling audiences and with the default of a trusted associate who had embezzled thirty thousand dollars from the company.[12] Charges were not brought against the man. After the company declared bankruptcy, Morley assumed personal liability for loans made to it; thus he experienced not only deep discouragement, but also considerable financial hardship. Out of this period of personal reexamination came *John Mistletoe*, Morley's thinly fictionalized autobiography, published in 1931.

The Roslyn War Memorial Building became the scene of Christopher Morley's second dramatic enterprise when he joined Broadway producer David Lowe in 1940 in organizing the Millpond Playhouse.[13] This local theater presented numerous plays, including Morley's *The Trojan Horse*, which enjoyed a two-month run. Both in emulation of Shakespeare and as an expression of his own involvement in the theater, Morley occasionally moved into acting parts himself at the Millpond Playhouse. He appeared in many of his own plays as well as in those of others such as Thornton Wilder's *Our Town*, in which Morley played the part of Stage Manager.

Christopher Morley's active career and involvement in Roslyn affairs began to slow after his first stroke in 1951, which temporarily paralyzed his right arm and hand. Only one volume of poems, *Gentlemen's Relish,* appeared between that time and his death on March 28, 1957. Along with his enormous corpus of works spanning over forty years, Morley left a wife and four children; one of his daughters published a novel in 1948.[14] Christopher Morley's career was unique among all American men of literature in this century in the variety of his literary activities — and, as an examination into his life shows, he was especially unusual because of his passionate involvement in the promotion of other authors and their works.

III   *Morley as Literary Promoter*

As to my speculations, there is little to admire in them but my admiration of others.

— William Hazlitt (Quoted by Morley)[15]

Whatever Christopher Morley was doing, he was certain to grab at any opportunity to promote his favorite authors. One of the tenets of his literary career, in fact, is illustrated by a newspaper clipping of a phrase of William Bolitho's which Morley tucked into his pocket diary for 1930: "Not to seek smartness by hiding enthusiasm."[16] This passion for promotion was constant throughout Morley's career, and it can be traced in virtually all of his literary activities. Appropriately, Morley's first job was with Doubleday and Company where from 1913 until 1917 he read manuscripts, promoted Doubleday authors, and visited booksellers personally as a salesman. Starting in the publicity department where he compiled "Literary Notes" to be sent to reviewers, Morley served both in and out of bookstores — he augmented the staffs of the Old Corner Bookstore in Boston and the Lord and Taylor Book Shop in New York during several Christmas seasons — and tried to create interest in overstocked books among buyers for chain stores. Reading manuscripts for the editorial department, Morley successfully pleaded for a number of them in council meetings. It is revealing to note that, prior to the publication of *Parnassus on Wheels* in 1917, he had already written one work concerned with booksellers: *The Bookseller's Blue Book,*[17] published in 1914. This work was strictly a trade publication that boosted Doubleday offerings.

While at Doubleday Morley earned a reputation as a tenacious fighter for authors whom he believed were being neglected; Doubleday, himself, recounts how, at every staff meeting for one period of months, ". . . when it came Christopher's turn to speak he always began, 'Now, about McFee — we don't appreciate what a comer he is,' and so on for five minutes without taking breath until finally it became the joke of the meeting that nothing could be done until Morley's McFee speech had been made. Our jibes influenced him not at all. His only reply to our efforts in humor being to bring on a look of great seriousness and the eternal phrase, 'Now, about McFee.'"[18] The book of William McFee's which so impassioned Morley was entitled *Casuals of the Sea;* and, when Doubleday had finally surrendered to Morley and published the work, it became both an artistic and financial success. Telling tales of the sea, an enduring Morley love, *Casuals of the Sea* remained one of his favorite books for many years.

Another Morley *cause célèbre* at Doubleday was Joseph Conrad. While the flavor of the sea contributed to his admiration for Conrad, he also recognized the depth of Conrad's themes. First introduced to Conrad's works by a talk given at Oxford in 1911 by Sir Sidney Colvin to a literary group of which Morley was a member, Morley felt that ". . . perhaps more than any other writer I can think of Conrad is (to me) valuable for self-discovery. . . . I read him to find out what is happening to myself."[19] Morley's influence was crucial in publishing Conrad's works in American editions; and in 1914 he was responsible for the separate publication of Conrad's suppressed "Preface" to *The Nigger of the Narcissus.*

When Morley left Doubleday to begin his career as a columnist, he continued his publicizing activities in the avenues opened by his new job. Morley edited many anthologies of the works of other writers, hoping to bring their works to a wider audience, and simultaneously developing for himself a considerable reputation as an editor. His first important venture in the field was *Modern Essays*.[20] After a lively and well-written introduction that offered prefatory remarks on each author, Morley presented his highly individual selection, including such personal friends as Don Marquis, Robert Cortes Holliday, David Bone, William McFee, H. M. Tomlinson, Heywood Broun, and Simeon Strunsky, as well as contemporary writers he admired, like Joseph Conrad, Hilaire Belloc, Rupert Brooke, George Santayana, Stephen Leacock, and Logan Pearsall Smith.

The success of this collection made possible a second series of *Essays* in 1924. The new selection contained only one writer included in the first volume, Stephen Leacock; for Morley now covered C. E. Montague, Henry Seidel Canby, Willa Cather, Alice Meynell, John Crowe Ransom, and Sherwood Anderson, among others. An abridged version of the first series was issued in 1922 as *Modern Essays for Schools*,[21] one of the first collections of contemporary essays for young readers.

Morley's next anthology was *The Bowling Green*, published in 1923 when he left his *New York Evening Post* column of that title.[22] Collecting some of the best verse and essays from the column, the list of contributors includes Hilaire Belloc, William Rose Benét, Stephen Vincent Benét, Edna St. Vincent Millay, and Elinor Wylie, as well as many lesser-known writers. *A Book of Days*, a collection of a different sort, contains 365 interesting quotations chosen by Morley from some of his favorite writers; his selections stress the importance of the individual, as well as delight in the pleasures of life.[23]

For the first National Book Fair in 1936 Morley compiled a souvenir book comprising short excerpts about books, reading, and authors; he again drew heavily on the works of fellow writers.[24] *Inward Ho!*, a small volume of his own essays, contains a remarkable appendix which Morley described as "a brief and rigorous anthology of comments on kindred matters."[25] And at the end of *Ex Libris Carissimis*, a group of his lectures published in 1932, Morley inserted a list of his own favorite books, which he called "Golden Florins." These included a number of Conrad selections; "anything" by Robert Louis Stevenson; several volumes of poems by his friend and

Saturday Review associate Elinor Wylie; Walt Whitman's entire works, poetry and prose; and the inevitable William McFee.[26] Although this group is a kind of congress of Morley favorites, many other less frequently publicized authors also appear in "Golden Florins."

While the majority of Christopher Morley's newspaper and magazine columns were not written as promotion for other writers, a great many of them were; and this intent is reflected in the volumes of essays that Morley published. Besides containing a major article about Don Marquis, *Shandygaff*, Morley's first volume of essays, includes articles about Rupert Brooke, Hilaire Belloc, and two about William McFee. The Brooke article is a typical specimen of Morley's unusual promotional techniques: he offers biographical notes about Rupert Brooke combined with selections from his poetry and with Morley's critical commentary. Excerpts range from Brooke's most famous lines,

> If I should die, think only this of me:
> That there's some corner of a foreign field
> That is for ever England[27]

to portions of lesser-known works which Morley particularly recommends to the reader. Morley successfully relates Brooke's poetry to the World War I environment in which he wrote: "It is no mere flippancy to say that the War did much for Rupert Brooke. The boy who had written many hot, morbid, immature verses and a handful of perfect poetry, stands now by one swift translation in the golden cloudland of English letters. There will never, can never, be any laggard note in the praise of his work. And of a young poet dead one may say things that would be too fulsome for life."[28] In addition to frequent and appropriate citations from Brooke's poetry, Morley includes in his essay not only his own flattering remarks but also the praise of other critics, including Gilbert Murray.

Later volumes of Morley's essays continued the practice of promoting authors, living and dead, as well as particular books that Morley felt deserved wider public exposure. If it was somewhat unusual that he spent so much time promoting decidedly minor figures, the issue never disturbed him: "When I say a 'minor favorite' I do so deliberately; some of the most exquisite pleasures of print are to be found in pursuit of the smaller names."[29] Morley therefore spent a significant percentage of his written space in the service of writers both famous and unknown, rightly believing that he was providing a valuable service to the author, and, more importantly, to the reader. In *The Powder of Sympathy* Morley writes of such luminaries as George Santayana (who was also the subject of several Morley reviews published in the Book-of-the-Month Club News) and De Quincey, but he also includes more personal favorites like Kenelm Digby and George Gissing. *The Romany Stain* contains a piece entitled "Jamie Comes to Hy-Brasil," which is a skillful promotional article on James Stephens' *In The Land of Youth;* "Every Tuesday" focuses on the works of John Donne, but manages to work in flattering comparisons with Sherwood Anderson and with friend Elinor Wylie. "Storms and Calms," in the same volume, successfully promotes Conrad's *The Shadow Line,* and it includes Morley's futile confession that "It is foolish of me to write about Conrad; and certainly I should never try to prejudice readers in favor of trying one special book before another."[30] Realizing the limitations of his promotions, however, never prevented Christopher Morley from continuing them.

IV   *Objects of Promotion*

Several authors acted as permanent fixed stars in Morley's galaxy and received public homage from him throughout his career. Robert Louis Stevenson was Morley's first real literary love: in his college days he wrote what was perhaps his first promotional essay about Stevenson's letters,[31] and he also wrote his senior thesis about Stevenson. At Oxford, the influence continued; and Morley read a paper on Stevenson to the Oxford American Club; as late as 1936 he included an essay about book collecting, which focused on Stevenson, in a volume of essays.[32]

A very special category should be imagined to describe the promotional essays Morley wrote about Don Marquis, for he was also one of Morley's closest friends, a sometime mentor, and the object of a continuing crusade by Morley to award him greater literary status than seemed to have been given him. Twelve years older than Morley, Marquis began his immensely popular *Sun Dial* column in the *New York Evening Sun* in 1912; it was to serve as Christopher Morley's inspiration when he began his own career as a newspaperman. In fact, it is clear that Morley began as an uncritical, hero-worshipping disciple of Don Marquis. In an essay published in *Shandygaff* in 1918 Morley adopts the promotional tone common in his writings about many other authors; but this tribute is filled with unusual and excessive intensity: "He stands out as one of the most

penetrating satirists and resonant scoffers at folderol that this conti-
nent nourishes. He is far more than a colyumist: he is a poet — a
kind of Meredithian Prometheus chained to the roar and clank of a
Hoe Press. He is a novelist of Stocktonian gifts. . . ."[33] This essay
offers many clever anecdotes about Marquis that are interspersed
with frequent quotations from his poetry and prose; it is interesting
to remember that the essay was written for one of Morley's own
newspaper columns, for it deals at some length with the difficulties
of column writing. Commiserating with Don Marquis, Morley muses
"I suppose that the conductor of a daily humorous column stands in
the hierachy of unthanked labourers somewhere between a plumber
and submarine trawler."[34] Morley makes sure that, in his column, at
least, Marquis is not allowed to go unthanked.

This example is by no means Morley's only tribute in column form
to Don Marquis; for it is a rare volume of Morley essays that omits
some reference to the humorist. *The Romany Stain*, a collection of
Morley's columns in *The Saturday Review* published in 1926, dis-
cusses the attempt of Morley and Marquis to produce a book in
collaboration in "The Middle Country Road."[35] Morley's last
volume of essays, *The Ironing Board*, recollects that "Don Marquis
said I must join the Mummers. That was a club of actors and writers
and boblishers."[36] This last word is typical of the linguistic puns and
creations that Morley enjoyed using throughout his career;
"boblishers," according to Morley, are publishers who always follow
the line of least sales resistance, while true publishers make "some
attempt to keep alive their author's most genuinely significant work;
not necessarily that which happened to win soft approval."[37]

During a 1937 lecture at the University of Michigan Morley spoke
feelingly and with a more mature critical sense about Marquis when
he compared him to Mark Twain; in the process, he indicated the
central problem of Marquis's career: "A writer who fulfills with
singular exactness the most vital native tradition of American letters,
whose grotesque and ironic humor was often put in parables too
blunt for intellectuals to perceive; a man whose work bears on almost
every page the stigmata of its origin, conceived under compulsion,
blotted before the ink was dry. . . ."[38] Late in his career Marquis
developed a yearning to write just one masterpiece that would win
him genuine fame and that would reflect all the ability he had
developed in his years of column writing. As Christopher Morley put
it, "Don had been planning and practising for this larger stroke in
fiction, and pushing toward it under duress of taskwork."[39]

Morley sympathized with the pressures under which Marquis had to operate; he wrote, in a column devoted to Don Marquis: "I'm sure dear old Dr. Johnson, as he ground away at his *Lives of the Poets*, cursed them as hackwork; yet in every paragraph they show the volume and pressure of that leviathan intelligence, breaching in the white foam of humor. So it was with Don Marquis . . . who created something utterly his own. It was as racy of our day as Addison and Steele's *Spectator* of theirs."[40] While Marquis did not lead so diversified a career as Morley, Don Marquis did assume many roles as a writer. He wrote both serious and humorous verse, several plays, a number of short stories, several novels, and many columns. Thus Morley was heir to many of the problems of writing that Marquis had faced, albeit not to the same degree. Morley theorized in one essay that one of the reasons Marquis's poetry had gained little critical recognition was that "he has puzzled the critics by writing verse of so many different kinds."[41] This comment is simultaneously a reference to Morley's own diverse writings, which may have made him equally suspect to many critics. Thus, by promoting and apologizing for Don Marquis so frequently and so enthusiastically, Morley may have been, on one level, attempting to explain some of the problems of his own career.

Another of the most heavily publicized residents of Morley's columns was Walt Whitman. Morley wrote laudatory prefaces to two volumes of Whitman's works, one strictly prose, and noted in his last volume of essays that "What an author takes the trouble to publish twice is important to him."[42] Morley was talking there about Whitman, but he might as easily have been discussing his own works about Whitman. *Walt* is an unambitious one-act play that Morley wrote about Whitman's last days. While outwardly very different, Morley and Whitman correspond deeply in certain respects: each viewed America as a land with many faults, but also as one with incredible potentialities, and both wrote with excessive enthusiasm occasionally. Morley admired the unbridled ego present in Whitman's writing — the fact that Whitman was as enthusiastic a publicizer of himself as Morley was of others: "I suppose no writer was ever so busy composing blurbs for himself, writing notices of his own books and ingeniously getting them into print."[43] While Whitman "celebrated himself," Morley achieved satisfaction both through his own works and through his services to other writers; his happiness lay, at least partially, in knowing that he was serving literature.

V *Promotional Advertising*

In one of the volumes that issued out of Morley's ill-fated Hoboken theater experiment, he inserted a collection of the very clever and effective advertisements that the group of entrepreneurs had placed in New York newspapers. These included such quips as "Save this notice, we can't afford to advertise much," which led E. E. Calkins to comment "I am not sure that Morley qualifies as an amateur in the field of advertising."[44] One of the items that created this suspicion in Calkins's mind was a skillful spoof of the advertising business called "Ginger Cubes," which Morley included in *The Powder of Sympathy*. This effort is presented in the form of an exchange of letters between a company president and his advertising manager, and includes several extended passages mocking the "rules of good advertising."[45]

Even Christopher Morley's novels were occasionally used as vehicles for publicity notes that refer to his close friends. *Rudolph and Amina*, adapted by Morley from a nineteenth-century melodrama and an otherwise uninteresting work, contains several references to the noted American book collector, A. W. Rosenbach, whom Morley finally brings in as a character.[46] (William Hulbert Footner, another friend of Morley's, managed to turn the tables on him in *The Mystery of the Folded Paper*, in which one Christopher Morley appears in an active role.[47]) Especially in his later years, Morley wrote numerous obituaries for fellow writers; in these he usually managed to plug either their best or their most neglected works, depending on Morley's perception of which most needed promotion.

Except for his largely editorial duties with the Book-of-the-Month Club, Christopher Morley's formal ties with the bookselling industry were severed in 1917 when he left Doubleday. Nevertheless, he maintained healthy relationships with the vendors of his favorite product in a number of ways. In some cases, he ordered private printings of his works for distribution to booksellers. One example of this procedure is the "dummy" edition of *Kitty Foyle* (containing only the first chapter) that was issued before publication in limited numbers.[48] When his last novel, *The Man Who Made Friends With Himself*, was published in 1949, Morley had sixteen hundred copies of a "private edition" printed for distribution to booksellers; it contained several significant additions to the regular edition.[49] In fact, as a book collector himself, Morley was especially conscious of bibliographic peculiarities; he regarded them as another valuable aspect of literary culture. He acted as contributing editor of *Colophon*, a book collector's quarterly magazine.[50] Morley also maintained close personal relationships with several booksellers, carrying on correspondence with some of them. These contacts not only aided the promotion of his own and his friends' publications, but also assisted him in setting up remunerative lecture tours.[51]

Not all of Morley's promotional activities were quite so organized, for Norman Cousins tells how Morley persuaded a stenographer at *The Saturday Review* offices to read Francis Thompson's essay about Shelley; Morley was "entranced the next day when, wide-eyed and converted, she asked for more. It was clear to him that she had experienced the shock of cognition; he concluded that he had helped to make a better world."[52] Publishers sought him for the introductions and prefaces they wanted, knowing that he could infect browsing readers with the desire to purchase a book they had only meant to peruse. Yet this enthusiasm was an honest one: Morley's preface to Charles Dickens's *The Cricket on the Hearth* was never used by the publisher who commissioned it because Morley had spoken too frankly of the book's weaknesses.

These varied promotional activities, ranging from serious essays, to idle conversation, to actual sales of books, reflect one of the central factors in Christopher Morley's attitude toward literature. He regarded the opportunity to foster previously undiscovered writing talent as an exciting chance to contribute to literary life that was beyond the scope of his own writing; more significantly, all of his words and deeds lead to the conclusion that Morley saw the roles of publisher, bookseller, and publicity agent as roughly equal in importance in the world of letters to that of the author. All were really "handmaidens" for the ideas and the beauty that books transmitted to the reader. Morley firmly rejected any hierarchy that separated the "artist" from those whose work was equally essential if art were to be made real and alive — if it were to find an audience to enjoy and appreciate it. His attitude thus stands in sharp contrast to those who consider advertising and promotion demeaning chores and who prefer to isolate themselves in pursuit of their own masterpieces. For a practicing, professional writer Christopher Morley's attitudes were certainly unusual, and perhaps unique.

Therefore, his extensive writing as a publicist should not be treated as a "commercial" or non-literary episode in his career as a writer. Rather, it is the logical, natural complement to all that he wrote and said about literature, as well as to the body of literary works that he produced himself. Christopher Morley believed that any work that furthered the spread and development of the literary art was thereby endowed with special dignity and significance, and this dignity is present in his essays, his novels, and his poems, as well as in his personal efforts as a publicist. The works and life of Christopher Morley form an understandable and coherent whole only if Morley is viewed as he saw himself — as a Literary Man.[53]

CHAPTER 2

Columns and Essays

I The Living Essay

ALTHOUGH Christopher Morley liked to speak of himself primarily as a poet, he believed by the last years of his life that his essays best exemplified his gifts as a writer. In his last volume of essays, published two years before his first stroke virtually ended his active writing career, Morley spoke ironically of himself: "He has been told, almost often enough to believe it, that he is not a novelist, nor a dramatist, nor a poet. But there is, maybe, a kind of satiric saltarello that is natural to his temper."[1] This comment does not indicate that Morley looked down upon essay writing, nor that he thought it an occupation beneath his dignity. In a reminiscent mood, Morley wrote in 1949:

There was a club once (about 33 years ago), that had only two members. . . . It was the Porrier's Corner Club near Doubleday's Press on Long Island. It was a saloon where Robert Cortes Holliday and I used to have a shell of beer (we could afford only one apiece) on our way home from work. We used to talk about Literature, which we loved and in our humble ways sued. We talked about George Gissing and Richard Jeffries, about Don Marquis and Simeon Strunsky, and all the gorgeous things that young men in publishing houses talk about. . . . One day an old man, I bet he was over fifty, who had been watching our antics, doddered up to us and said, "What do you boys talk about all the time? The Death of the Essay?"

"Mister," we cried, "them's fighting words!"[2]

His essays appeared most frequently in *The Saturday Review of Literature*, but Morley was a frequent contributor to numerous other publications in the United States and Great Britain. By 1922 he had "escaped into print"[3] in the *Philadelphia Public Ledger*, the *New York Evening Post*, and the *Atlantic Monthly*.[4] A 1936 volume contained selections from *The Saturday Review,* a preface, a radio broadcast, and a piece composed for an anthology of "personal candors."⁵ Another volume contained pieces written for *Coronet Magazine, The Bookman,* and *The Commonweal,* plus a preface for a new edition of *Dreamthorp* by Alexander Smith.⁶ Later essays appeared in *The New Colophon, '47 Magazine, Ellery Queen's Mystery Magazine, London Mystery Magazine,* the *Manchester Guardian,* the *Baker Street Journal, Life Magazine,* the *Philadelphia Inquirer,* and the *New York Herald Tribune.*⁷ Occasional essays appeared in *The American Mercury.*⁸

Morley's essays can be conveniently divided into several descriptive categories that possess more than purely descriptive force. The first of these is the promotional essay, which we have already dealt with in some detail. A closely related genre is Morley's "literary" essay in which he often reacted personally to a particular book or to an incident which recalled some book to him. Frequently, these essays were directed into Morley's favorite channel of thought — the relationships between literature and life. Another major category of Morley's essays is the literary travelogue, in which the travelling or reminiscing Morley explores places associated with great or with simply interesting events in the history of English literature.

Most of these essays were composed for immediate publication in one of the newspapers or magazines for which Morley wrote columns. In fact, until he left the *New York Evening Post* in 1924, Morley considered himself primarily a journalist; he was writing short stories about the daily problems of newspapermen as well as dealing with them in his essays. Once he had completed his novel, *Where the Blue Begins,* in 1922, however, Morley increasingly desired to quit the world of journalism. In that year he noted in his journal that "it's pretty nearly time to pull up stakes and cleave to the perdurable stuff before the mere journalism becomes a habit." Although he had resolved in June, 1922, to quit the *Post* by February of the following year, it was not until December that he severed the connection. During 1923, though, Morley had made his desire evident by declining Ellery Sedgwick's offer to become his associate in editing *The Atlantic Monthly.*⁹

After his departure from the *Post* Morley wrote a finely crafted extended essay, *Religio Journalistici,* as a bittersweet farewell to the newspaper business. "A little pride," he reminded his fellow workers, "is desirable now and then; yes, in God's name, a little pride, gentlemen." Not one to disparage the journalist, Morley in later life continued to show a sincere if somewhat cautious respect for the functions of the daily newspaper. While no longer formally connected with any newspaper after 1923, Morley retained something of the reporter in his make-up, as well as in that of his columns. For example, when he was the subject of interviews, he was apt to try to turn the tables on the reporters by asking them questions.

Morley recognized the limitations of journalism, despite his love for the culture that surrounded it: "To belittle newspapers for not telling the truth is as silly as to regard them as training ground for literature. Literature and journalism rarely overlap."[10] When he was free of the demands of daily newspaper work, Morley began to concentrate more heavily on his literary efforts; it is clear, however, that he never lost his journalistic instincts. A contemporary critic remarked of Morley's writing that, "even if some of it had been done as part of a journalist's regular job, he had put his heart as well as his mind into it and found pleasure in the doing."[11]

II   *The Literary Essay*

Christopher Morley's essays remained essentially journalistic, for he relied on the highly developed format that he had perfected early in his career. Of course, given the larger space allotted to his magazine columns than his newspaper ones had ever warranted, and the less frequent deadlines, his work became more literary in tone, more highly polished. The pattern Morley followed was, above all, quite personal: he talked exclusively either of things that had happened to him or of the people and the places that caught his fancy at a particular moment. Since he was involved with many of the important literary personages and events of his day, these personal essays often gained additional interest for his readers beyond Morley's own style and charm. In his introduction to a volume of *Leaves of Grass* which he edited, Morley attributed some of his intense personalism to Whitman's influence:

Like everyone who has rudiments of decent reticence I used to feel bashful about the exciting things that happened to *me*. I thought it was perhaps weird or ominous that such intricately ironic or amusing or painful seizures should take hold of a spirt so well-meaning and obscure. This must have happened to all who still struggle bravely against the rigors of taught and inherited manners. To confide too much of what one really feels might seem like vanity, or ill breeding. Worse, it might be tedious, and the occasion of eliciting wearisome confession from others. The very first thing one learns from Walt is that a certain amount of candor about one's private emotions may be not egotism but humility. It does not divide one from humanity at large but brings the comforting assurance that all men suffer and enjoy much alike. Therefore Walt encourages me, as he has encourged every other who ever got friendly with his writings, to be personal.[12]

His own very immediate and personal reactions to walking the dog, taking a stroll in the woods, rediscovering an old favorite book, visiting the home of a great author — these were the raw materials for Christopher Morley's essays for more than thirty years.

A fine example of the Morley "literary" essay is "Trivia," which appeared in *Shandygaff*. It opens with a sociological observation rather than with a literary comment:

> The bachelor is almost extinct in America. Our hopelessly utilitarian civilization demands that a man of forty should be rearing a family, should go to an office five times a week, and pretend an interest in the World's Series. It is unthinkable to us that there should be men of mature years who do not know the relative batting averages of the Red Sox and the Pirates. The intellectual and strolling male of from thirty-five to fifty-five years (which is what one means by bachelor) must either marry and settle down in the Oranges, or he must flee to Europe or the MacDowell Colony. There is no alternative. Vachel Lindsay please notice.[13]

After bemoaning the loss of "these quaint, phosphorescent middle-aged creatures,"[14] including such notables as Henry James, Morley notes that England still offers a haven for bachelors. In fact, because the one particular refugee bachelor whom Morley intends to discuss is Logan Pearsall Smith, Morley's amusing dissertation on bachelors was merely a means of preparing his readers for some literary education. For several pages he discourses about *Trivia*, Pearsall Smith's collection of essays which Morley calls "a bright tissue of thought robing a radiant, dancing spirit."[15] Having quoted several intriguing passages from *Trivia*, Morley tries to place it in literary perspective by comparing Smith's work to such diverse writers as Marcus Aurelius and Harold Bell Wright. His serious work done, Morley reverts back to his lament for the fate of bachelors in America. He uses Pearsall Smith as an example of what we have lost through our intolerance, closing with a humorous anecdote. Under the guise of social comment and storytelling, Morley has talked to his readers about his most constant subject, literature.

This systematic concealment of his more serious purposes characterizes many of Christopher Morley's essays. In his late volume entitled *Streamlines* Morley hides a discussion of the philosophy in Laurence Sterne's *Tristram Shandy* behind a chatty essay about the typographical techniques and problems involved in the novel.[16] "Matthew Arnold and Exodontia," in *The Powder of Sympathy*, combines excerpts from Arnold's work with a trip to the dentist; for example, this transition is cleverly handled: "You probably thought (and justly) that we cut off Matthew Arnold rather abruptly yesterday. Well, we did; but there's always a reason for everything. We had to hurry uptown, by order of Dr. James Kendall Burgess, the philosophical dentist, to call on Dr. Hillel Feldman for some exodontia. In the old days, we dare say, it would have been called having a tooth pulled, but we like the word exodontia much better."[17]

After he has finished narrating his visit to Dr. Feldman, Morley draws the two subjects together, permitting himself to return once more to Matthew Arnold, his real subject: "Matthew Arnold, as we were saying, complained that American civilization was not *interesting*. A silly thing to say, it seems to us. He meant, evidently, that it did not supply the kind of interest to which he was accustomed, or for which he yearned. For surely, to any one ready to lay aside preconceptions, *interesting* is exactly what American life has always been. We reflected that the one word we instinctively used in explaining to Dr. Feldman how we had enjoyed our visit to him was just that — interesting."[18]

Christopher Morley has made literature painless with his anesthetic of anecdote and wit. Again, in "Goodbye to Spring," which appeared in *Letters of Askance*, Morley begins with a few observations about the arrival of summer, but he soon digresses to quotations from a book announcement that he has just read, and eventually to quotations from A. E. Housman's *Last Poems*.[19] By recounting casually and easily the small events that caught his fancy, Morley was able to write serious literary essays which attracted his readers and kept their attention.

III   *Literature and Life*

A large number of Christopher Morley's essays deal more or less explicitly with the relationships he found between literature and life. In one essay he confessed that "I find it harder and harder to know where literature ends and life begins."[20] This line of thought produced essays such as "The Material to the Artist" in *The Romany Stain*, which draws an equivalency between artistry in life and in creative work.[21] "The Palette Knife," which gives an impressionistic "painter's eye-view" of Long Island Sound, concludes, "What brush, what dear childish pigments, can be pointed sharp enough for that? Oils and paints and colours are only a medium — something in between. A haze, a web, a shadow between us and the dark sea of words in which the mind must live. We swim black shoreless waters where every stroke is sluiced with goblin fire."[22]

Reflecting both the attitudes and style of Joseph Conrad, this passage helps explain Morley's deep affection for the works of that writer. "Carrier Pigeons," a lecture published as an essay in *Ex Libris Carissimis*, opens in Morley's typically offhand manner:

> I want to tell you a little story of how life comes to heel after literature. The theme, if any, of these afternoons really is the inextricable interweaving of life and literature and the truth that literature is embedded in life and can't be put into textbooks and analyzed and discussed as though it were a laboratory process. . . .
>
> Now, the coincidence which I laboriously approach came about as follows: I had written a few days before to a friend of mine on the staff of the Oxford University Press, saying that I had heard of this new edition of selections from Fuller, and that when it came to Thomas Fuller, I was the original Fuller Brush Man. I apologize for that, it was a cheap witticism, and particularly so because the phrase, "The Fuller Brush Man," meant nothing to me; it was one of those random words that I had heard vaguely without knowing just what it meant or where it came from. . . . I didn't know anything about Fuller brushes, and the Fuller Brush Man himself might have lived anywhere from Maine to Manila, as far as I knew or cared. So I sat in the train from New Haven northward, reading Thomas Fuller and joying in his exquisite felicities. I laid down the book at one moment, transfixed by some particularly lovely paragraph of his . . . and glanced out of the window; and just at that exact instant, not more than a second's duration, the one instant when it might have happened in that whole journey, just north of Hartford, as I looked out of the window there was the Fuller Brush Factory.
>
> I admit it is not very important, but I felt it was magic. That is the way life comes to heel after literature.[23]

This essay is but one excellent example of Morley's conviction that what is apparently coincidental in life is really pregnant with meaning — that life often patterns itself after literature; Northup Frye calls this phenomenon "the literesque." Or, as Christopher Morley put it elsewhere, "whenever one says, 'It *would* be like that, it *would* happen to *me*,' one makes instinctive admission of the contriving art-spirit of the world."[24]

The small collection called *Inward Ho!* is one of the most serious and sustained efforts that Morley produced to document the relationship between literature and life. This volume is often aphoristic, full of such lines as "Perhaps, therefore, man's weaknesses are due to inbreeding, Art and Nature being too closely kin."[25] Fifteen essays, each exploring a different aspect of Christopher Morley's love for and involvement with literature, are concluded with a collection of remarks by such writers as Yeats, Keats, Sandburg, Tolstoy, Bacon, and Whitman on similar topics. It is initially astonishing that these very personal and intimate essays were first written as columns in the *New York Evening Post* in 1923.

IV   The Spirit of Place

In addition to his concern with the literature-life question, Christopher Morley was also obsessed by his sense of place, both by the "spirit of place,"[26] which he found in particular locations, and by the physical environments involved in the world of literature. In *John Mistletoe* Morley claimed that, "To be deeply rooted in a place that has meaning is perhaps the best gift a child can have."[27] One of his first volumes of essays, *Travels in Philadelphia,* a collection of columns written for the *Philadelphia Evening Public Ledger,* was a sort of journal of life in Philadelphia as Morley saw it. Morley's love for the obscure but interesting corners of a city that is not known for its excitements is sympathetically and anecdotally explored. A number of Philadelphia scenes stand out vividly: a visit to Whitman's house in Camden; the description of "Martha Washington," the Independence Hall cat; an account of being "bullied by the birds" in a Philadelphia suburb. One Philadelphia landmark that Morley showed special fondness for was Dooner's, the tavern that he used for several scenes in *Kitty Foyle.* The bright descriptions of Philadelphia's "Little Italy" demonstrate Morley's fondness for newly immigrant peoples, as well as his preference for the individual and the variegated, as opposed to the collective and the homogeneous.

When Morley moved to New York City, he continued this place-centered writing on a larger scale. He developed favorite symbols of New York life, such as the statue of Diana that stood above Madison Square Garden and that came to stand for Morley's image of New York as the perfect mistress for the artist, ever-challenging and inspiring. Morley discussed the statue in many essays; and, when Diana was removed from her perch, he wrote "The Constant Nymph" as a lament.[28] Speaking of the "fascination of the physically actual in literature," Morley tried to explain why he wrote so passionately about the many small places which made up his New York: "Things sometimes do not seem to have any spiritual existence until they have been written about. I myself, because they mean so much to me, jabber about Vesey Street, St. Paul's Churchyard, the Telephone and Telegraph Building, the old courtyard on Ann Street, a hundred other minutiae of that region, because I yearn to help them along toward that splendid significance they desire."[29] Knowing how quickly the city changed, Morley hoped to record at least a small portion of what made Manhattan important to him. From McSorley's Saloon to the New York subway, Morley tried to capture in his essays the people and places that mattered to him, and he wrote of them with respect and affection.

One of Morley's frequent goals in his essays was to present a clear picture of Long Island, and of the village of Roslyn in particular, to his readers and their posterity. Rarely calling it by name, Morley wrote many times about Roslyn as "Salamis" during the thirty-seven years that he lived there. Many details of the Long Island countryside — for Roslyn in the 1920's was more rural than urban — appeared in Morley's essays, which expressed his interest in human life in all its various manifestations. Christopher Morley felt at home, and therefore genuinely free, in widely divergent locales.

V   *Literary Travelogues*

This sense of place expressed itself more often, however, in Morley's "literary travelogue" essays. A trip to the Caribbean resulted in "Notes on Bermuda," the summer spent in France in 1924 gave him material for many of the essays in *The Romany Stain*, and a visit to Peru produced not only the book-length, if trivial, *Hasta la Vista*, but also an essay entitled "South American Pilot." Additional opportunities for travel were given Morley by the numerous lecture trips he made in the 1930's, which he called "... exhausting, but the most exciting way of seeing one's country (from Maine to Hawaii, from Toronto or Minneapolis to Texas or Atlanta) without debit. Even in spite of the autographing which could not be evaded without crudeness and rudeness, it was an immortal experience. I remember it with deep and humble gratitude...."[30]

A particular aspect of travel that Morley enjoyed and that was reflected in the essays was his love for ships. In language that was technically correct, yet still comprehensible to the layman, Morley gave detailed descriptions of voyages on the *Saxonia,* the *Caronia,* and the *Transylvania;* he described the arrival of the *Queen Mary* and the landing of the *Aquitania.* A long essay, "Off the Deep End," tells of a voyage to Halifax on a yacht, the *Iris.* Morley's writing about ships was based on solid knowledge gleaned from actual experience and from conversations with his friends Captain David Bone, Captain Felix Reisenberg, merchantman engineer William McFee, and ship news reporter Lawrence Perry.

Frequently, however, the point of Morley's travelogues was more literary. In "A Map of London" Morley takes the reader through a tour of London's landmarks of literary history, such as the Cheshire Cheese Pub, with extensive commentary on their places in the works of famous British writers.[31] "1941" begins as a visit to the battlefields of World War II; but, when it quickly becomes an essay about Shakespeare's *The Tempest,* it draws analogies between war, literature, and creativity.[32] In one of the earliest issues of *The Saturday Review* Morley began "The Benedictine Style" with comments about the French countryside and then developed a study of the French passion for linguistic perfection.[33] These essays were yet another way in which he concealed his serious literary purposes behind a more palatable screen — in this case, chatty travelogues. Other essays memorialized great days in literary history, such as the anniversary of Shelley's death by drowning, or spots where great writers such as Walt Whitman were born.

VI   *Self-Indulgent Essays*

Quite an appreciable number of Morley columns were book reviews, although often of a rather unique variety. Many begin with a short history of the circumstances through which Morley discovered the book — what book shop he was lazily exploring, for example, or which friend had sent him a copy. Conversely, a Morley review might start with a protest that a particular book had not been made sufficiently available to the general public, or at least to Morley. In a review of C. E. Montague's *Disenchantment,* a powerful critique of World War I, Morley complains "It is curious that the agencies for letting people know about the things that really matter are so feeble and ineffective. . . . They don't come very often, the books that speak so generously and beautifully to the inner certainties of the mind. . . . Well, the book, quietly written and published, turned out to be by Mr. Montague himself. Half a year went by, but we in America heard nothing about it."[34]

If a book was to Morley's liking, he usually spent some pages quoting it and praising it unstintingly. Reviewing Hilaire Belloc's *The Path to Rome*, Morley announced that "we find [in Belloc] the perfect union of the French and English minds. Rabelaisian in fecundity, wit, and irrepressible sparkle, he is also of English blood and sinew, wedded to the sweet Sussex weald. . . . It is in the essays, the thousand little inquirendoes into the nature of anything, everthing, or nothing, that one comes closest to the real man. His prose leaps and sparks from the pen."[35] However, if Morley felt that a work was pretentious, such as Rabindranath Tagore's philosophical treatises, he could be brutally satirical. "A Venture in Mysticism," published in *Shanygaff*, tells the sad story of an office worker who attempts to apply Tagore's meditative principles to his own life with disastrous consequences.[36] The forced sensitivity of Tagore directly conflicted with Morley's own natural curiosity and easily interested approach to life.

In other book reviews and essays Morley often explored those problems of literature and writing that directly concerned his own technique and style. For example, in a review of Logan Pearsall Smith's *The Prospects of Literature*, Morley wrote: "First, he says, in the great period of literary creation there was always an underlying body of fairly unanimous ideas about life. Rightly or wrongly, there were coherent and generally accepted notions about destiny, morality, and all the other abstractions and concepts. Men had a formula, an agreed convention, a complete scheme of things, *'which gave them that imaginative dominion over experience which produced greatness.'* (That, I think, deserves the italic.)"[37]

Morley later repeated the phrase in *John Mistletoe* in which he commented that "the chief necessity for the artist is 'imaginative dominion over experience.'"[38] Years later, speaking through the character of Richard Tolman, Morley announced that "I hope I sometimes have imaginative dominion over experience." It is evident that Morley was a writer who consciously sought to interpret the events of his life, rather than attempting research into historical fact or venturing into the realms of pure invention. Thus, throughout his life, Morley relied heavily on notes which he took of things he had thought, seen, or read; and he used these memoranda extensively in his writing. This note-taking habit only intensified his desire to observe, and his method eventually evolved into a pattern of observing; note-taking; revising at his suburban home on Tuesday, Thursday, and Saturday; and then dictating in his New York office on Monday, Wednesday, and Friday.[39]

One artistic problem which this reliance on his own experience forced Morley to confront, and which often surfaced in his essays, was the difficulty of drawing the line between egotism and humility. How much of his existence could be useful to his readers? At times, Morley felt that "the business of writing is solidly founded on a monstrous and perilous egotism. Himself, his temperament, his powers of observation and comment, his emotions and sensibilities and ambitions and idiocies — these are the only monopoly the writer has. This is his only capital, and with glorious and shameless confidence he proposes to market it."[40] Or, as Morley once expressed the same thought poetically,

> Cries the poet every day:
> *Ego, mei, mihi, me!*[41]

Conscious of the large role of egotism in the art of writing, Morley was deeply moved by these insightful lines by William Watson:

> Momentous to himself as I to me
> Hath each been that woman bore;
> Once in a lightning-flash of sympathy,
> I felt this truth, an instant, and no more.[42]

Here was one answer to Morley's dilemma: by writing of his own life, he also wrote for and to others. Walt Whitman, who had come to the same conclusion in his "Song of Myself," had insisted that "these are really the thoughts of all men in all ages and lands, they are not original with me./ If they are not yours as much as mine they are nothing, or next to nothing." Echoing Whitman's words, with which he was intimately familiar, Morley wrote in an autobiographical poem, "this 'I' is not just *Me*, but YOU."[43]

Despite his frequent travels, Morley was often introspective. This aspect of his life, and writing, is illustrated by a passage from Franz Kafka's *The Great Wall of China* which impressed Morley a great deal: "You do not need to leave your room. Remain sitting at your table and listen. Do not even listen, simply wait. Do not even wait, be quite simple and solitary. The world will freely offer itself to you to be unmasked, it has no choice, it will roll in ecstasy at your feet."[44]

Richard Tolman, in *The Man Who Made Friends With Himself*, is made to echo these sentiments: "It is what Kafka said. You don't need to stir from your place, wherever it is. Just sit there and watch; the world will roll with ecstasy at your feet." Morley's essays, whether outwardly concerned with travel or with contemplation, usually returned to some literary concern that he found intriguing.

Christopher Morley's columns and essays were, in this sense, literally self-indulgent: they dealt with things that genuinely interested Morley. In his college days Morley had discovered that he could talk about his own interests in a style that others found attractive; an essay on "The Limerick," written for his college literary magazine, was a gentle parody of literary critics, full of Morley's love of word games and etymologies.[45] Often his essays contained coinages of his own. "Kinsprit," an early Morleyism, combines "kindred" with "spirit."[46] A later bastardization of Greek and Latin roots was "infracaninophile," which very precisely means "One who sympathizes with under-dogs."[47] Morley was often so obsessively and excessively literate in his essays that he drove many conscientious readers to the dictionary more often than they might have liked. Henry Seidel Canby described this aspect of Morley as "Morley II, a bad boy of letters, a punster without restraint, whimsical, witty, using the oldest tricks as well as the newest inventions."[48]

Christopher Morley produced a whole series of detective story parodies interspersed throughout his volumes of essays, with literary agent Dove Dulcet acting the role of literary detective.[49] Morley's abiding interest in Sherlock Holmes reappears here: one Dulcet adventure is entitled "Murder in Red and Green," a title that is an obvious takeoff on Conan Doyle's "A Study in Scarlet."[50] The passion for Holmes surfaces again in Morley's occasional pieces of Sherlock Holmes "scholarship," often written for the *Baker Street Journal*. One such essay claimed to answer in the affirmative the question, "Was Sherlock Holmes an American?"[51] Yet another tried to solve the problem of Dr. Watson's marriages: while other Holmesians had been led by some remarks of Watson to postulate as many as three marriages by the doctor, Morley employed detailed textual exegesis to build a case for a single marriage.[52]

Always interested both in technological developments and in unconventional individuals, Morley wrote about, and eventually became close friends with, R. Buckminster Fuller. During the 1930's Fuller did not enjoy either the respect or the reputation with which he is endowed today; Fuller's schemes for transforming society through technology failed even to support him financially. Morley not only provided financial assistance to Fuller: he believed in his ideas and made significant efforts to promote them. His 1936 volume of essays, *Streamlines*, is dedicated to "Buckminster Fuller, scientific idealist."[53] The title is drawn from a Morley essay about Fuller which is subtitled "Thoughts in a Dymaxion Car" and which is accompanied by photographs of Fuller and his inventions. "Dymaxion," a term created by Fuller out of his favorite terms, "dynamism," "maximum," and "ions," expresses Fuller's basic principle of "maximum gain of advantage from minimal energy input."[54] The adjective appealed to Morley, himself the author of many uniquely expressive words. Morley's workshop, The Knothole, was furnished with one of Fuller's rare "Dymaxion Bathroom" units, a complete bathroom stamped and shaped in a production-line operation: it can still be examined in The Knothole in Christopher Morley Park, Long Island.

A unique and interesting extended essay of Morley's is *History of an Autumn,* an account of his reactions to the events in Europe in the closing months of 1938, climaxed by Chamberlain's trip to Munich. Noted historian Frederick Lewis Allen believed that the book captured "the way things looked then, and . . . how we felt about them."[55] Most notably, Franklin D. Roosevelt wrote to Morley to say, "I suppose that when one reads a little book and says to himself at the end 'That was my autumn, too,' the next step is to say 'How did that fellow, Christopher Morley, know it?' Shrewdly I suspect that there were a good many million Morleys and Roosevelts in the world that survived the same processes — but I am glad that one of them was able to put it into a little book."[56] *History of an Autumn,* really an impressionistic journal, mixes simple observation with attempts to draw meaning from the nearly incomprehensible events then occurring. Through it all, however, Morley's faith in his fellow humans and his sense of humor remained unshaken; discussing Hitler, Morley observes that "Everyone knows that the only way to deal with lunatics is to outsmart them with kidding."[57]

While Christopher Morley produced many of his essays at frequent intervals to meet publication deadlines and fill weekly columns, he does not ever seem to have felt the kind of oppression that dominated his friend Don Marquis; Morley's essays were not that "hackwork" to him that Marquis frequently felt his own columns to be; for Morley's were written as naturally as breathing or eating. Morley had a difficult time thinking of his casual writing as "work" or of himself as an "essayist." In an obituary essay for his friend, Robert Cortes Holliday, Morley was perhaps thinking about himself nearly as much as about Holliday: "If there is such a creature as an essayist, Bob was it. His mind calibrated in exactly that frequency. So he is luckier than less tightly modulated receivers, who go sprouting round among every kind of affiche."[58]

As one of those "less tightly modulated receivers," Morley spread his time and talent among many literary activities. He seemed to treat his poetry most seriously; he found his novels often the most difficult to write; his columns and essays, however, were often close to pure enjoyment for Morley, flowing from his pen with practiced ease. This same facility allowed him to conceal his literary publicizing, his philosophizing, and his frequent attempts to assist in the education of his readers beneath rich layers of wit and charm. While most of Christopher Morley's essays were written to be informative, they were always given the additional task of amusing and entertaining the reader: they constitute the shiniest, most polished surface of a many-faceted mind.

CHAPTER 3

Novels

C ONSIDERED as a group, the novels of Christopher Morley
   comprise a kind of biography of literary life during the first half
of the twentieth century. While not concerned with any particular
individuals prominent in American literature, they portray nearly all
aspects of the culture surrounding the production and distribution of
books in America. Most Morley novels of any significance contain at
least one character, usually the protagonist, who is involved directly
with books, magazines, and literature. This factor is both a reflection
of the world that Morley knew best and a projection of his dominant
interest in the people and institutions surrounding literature.
However, Morley's many novels are not merely paeans to books or
essays converted into fictional form; for, in his later novels especially, he developed acute characterizations and intricate plots. All
of the novels are concerned with people and the problems confront-
ing them at various periods of their lives. The constant presence of
literature is naturally explained in the context of Christopher
Morley's philosophy that literature and life are inextricably in-
terwoven; it is difficult for him to conceive of a life that is not concerned with books and writing; and it is equally hard for him to treat
literature in other than a living context.

I   Parnassus on Wheels *and* The Haunted Bookshop

Parnassus on Wheels, Morley's first novel, was published in 1917,
when he was twenty-seven; and, clearly a young man's book, it is
filled with optimism, exuberance, and pre-war innocence. The
narrative is about Roger Mifflin (undoubtedly of the Houghton
Mifflins), an itinerant bookseller who travels through the countryside in a horse-drawn van, the "Parnassus," and sells books to
farmers. He approaches his work with missionary fervor; and, when

he stops at the farm of Andrew McGill and his sister Helen (perhaps the offspring of a marriage between McGraw and Hill), he inspires Helen so thoroughly that she buys the "Parnassus" from him and takes it on the road. Her brother is disturbed by the loss of his cook and housekeeper, but Helen is not to be dissuaded from her newly found mission of bringing literature to the many book-starved farmers she meets during her journey. Along the way she becomes re-involved with Roger Mifflin; and, by the end of the novel, she has discovered that she is in love with him. Since the excitement of literature has also transformed her life, she will be a New England spinster no longer. While the romance unifies the book, most of its substance is supplied by Helen's encounters with her rural customers, as well as with the voluble Mifflin. Abrasive and persuasive, he is a memorable character as seen through Helen's eyes, and an ideal preacher of Morley's gospel of the importance of literature to life.

The tale was written, Morley has noted, when he was refused a twenty-dollar-a-week raise that he had asked for from Doubleday: "checked in this mounting ambition for the lucrative side of the business he became an author almost, as it were, in retaliation. What spare energy there was he bent on the composition of a harmless little tale about an itinerant book-seller. It was a very unpretentious romance and written in appropriately humble surroundings: in the kitchen of a happy cottage on the windy Hempstead Plains. The winter of 1915-16 was a cold one in that small frame dwelling, and to draw the table close to the kitchen stove was the best way to keep warm without unduly squandering the coal hoarded for the furnace."[1] It took Morley seven months to write the novel at night and in his spare time; it was rejected by *Every Week, Woman's Home Companion, Ladies Home Journal, Collier's,* and *American Magazine* before Doubleday, Page, after considering it for two months, finally accepted the manuscript in July, 1916. A cautious first printing of fifteen hundred copies was issued more than a year later.

The idea for *Parnassus on Wheels* came from Morley's encounter in the spring of 1914 with Ray Stannard Baker's *Adventures in Contentment,* one of a popular series of books purportedly by "David Grayson," a farmer-philosopher who recited his excitements with much sentiment and little humor. Grayson had a fictional sister, Harriet, whose side of the story is never told; and Morley had originally intended to open his book with a reference to Grayson's unused character. Early editions of *Parnassus on Wheels* are prefaced with "A Letter to David Grayson" in which Morley indicates some similarities between his characters and those of Baker.

Morley's character in the novel who corresponds with David Grayson is Andrew McGill. As presented by his sister Helen, the narrator, McGill is a lovable but slightly foolish man. Although he is occasionally referred to as "The Sage of Redfield," the books he is supposed to have written, such as *Happiness and Hayseed*, are not the sort we are likely to want to read, even though we are assured that his prose is very good.

Of the two books, both published by Doubleday, Morley's seems to have fared better over the years: *Parnassus on Wheels* has never been out of print, and total sales of it and its sequel, *The Haunted Bookshop*, now exceed 127,000 copies in several editions, the most recent issued in 1955.

Using a time-honored narrative device, Morley disclaims credit for the novel by informing us in a prefatory note that Helen "told me the story with her own inimitable vivacity." And it is Helen's honesty and strength that eventually win the reader. As she tells the story simply, she makes now and then small mistakes, reveals her lack of formal education, and shows homely interest in the cooking of her neighbors. She is also able to admit humorously her own limitations: when, toward the end of the book, Helen realizes how much she loves Roger Mifflin, she makes up a kind of chant which she calls "Hymn for a Middle-Aged Woman (Fat) Who Has Fallen into Love." Though uneducated, Helen is observant; she sees a tiny rim of new moon "like a thumbnail paring"; and she notices, when Roger is distraught, "a little sort of fairy ring of tiny drops around his crown." It is easy to sympathize with her latent feeling for beauty and poetry, which Mifflin and his literary preaching arouse.

While the characters are rather humorously drawn and while the romance between Helen McGill and Roger Mifflin provides much of the action, *Parnassus on Wheels* is filled with brave lines that proclaim Morley's philosophy of the importance of literature to the lives of ordinary people: " 'Lord!' he [Roger Mifflin] said, 'when you sell a man a book you don't sell him just twelve ounces of paper and ink and glue — you sell him a whole new life. Love and friendship and humour and ships at sea by night — there's all heaven and earth in a book, a real book I mean.' "[2]

Morley also uses the voice of Roger Mifflin to take friendly pokes at some of his favorite and famous predecessors: " 'The world is full of writers about literature,' he said, 'but they're all selfish and aristocratic. Addison, Lamb, Hazlitt, Emerson, Lowell — take any one you choose — they all conceive the love of books as a rare and perfect mystery for the few — a thing of the secluded study where they can sit alone at night with a candle, and a cigar, and a glass of port on the table and a spaniel on the hearthrug. What I say is, who has ever gone out into high roads and hedges to bring literature home to the plain man?' "[3]

This passage, coming at the beginning of Morley's long career, is a kind of Morley Manifesto, the statement of a theme which was to recur in his writings many times and which goes a long way toward explaining Morley's writings as well as his career. To make literature really alive and vital, says Morley, it must be infused into the life of the entire citizenry — not merely that of an intellectual clique. In all of his writing Christopher Morley tried to make the names, thoughts, and words of great writers familiar to his readers; and he believed that, in doing so, he was serving both literature and life.

Only once in his career did Christopher Morley produce a sequel to a successful novel: *The Haunted Bookshop* brings back Roger Mifflin and Helen McGill — now Mrs. Helen Mifflin — and introduces a few younger characters who are to be lectured to about the importance of books. No longer on the road, the Mifflins now operate a bookshop in Brooklyn, which coincidentally becomes involved in a German spy plot. Morley, not Helen, is the narrator of *The Haunted Bookshop*, but he places himself in the background so that Roger Mifflin can now emerge as the main character. Mifflin, indeed, dismisses Morley with dispatch: "A young journalist came to see us once, with very unhappy results. He wheedled himself into Mrs. Mifflin's good graces, and ended by putting us both into a book, called *Parnassus on Wheels*, which has been rather a trial to me. In that book he attributes to me a number of shallow and sugary observations upon bookselling that have been an annoyance to the trade. I am happy to say, though, that the book had only a trifling sale." Having sent Helen on a trip to Boston and having provided Roger Mifflin with "Parnassus at Home," a secondhand bookstore in Brooklyn replete with tobacco smoke, the odor of old leather and paper, and "a kind of drowsy dusk, stabbed here and there by bright cones of yellow light from green-shaded electrics," Morley, in turn-

ing the narrative over to Mifflin, gives rein through him to some of
his own enthusiasms.

Roger Mifflin is not a cipher; he is a unique, non-conforming person, even something of a social radical. And he has apparently come
to this fully developed state largely through reading good books. As
a result, he is essentially tolerant and optimistic, although Morley
notes that booksellers tend to be "possibly a trifle embittered, which
is an excellent demeanor for mankind in the face of inscrutable
heaven." Therefore, Mifflin can see a useful application for books to
the confused state of the world following the devastation, physical
and intellectual, wrought by World War I: " 'Do you know why people are reading more books now than ever before? Because the
terrific catastrophe of the war has made them realize that their
minds are ill. The world was suffering from all sorts of mental fevers
and aches and disorders, and never knew it. Now our mental pangs
are only too manifest. We are all reading, hungrily, hastily, trying to
find out — after the trouble is over — what was the matter with our
minds.' "[4]

In the course of an argument with Aubrey Gilbert, the young
advertising agent who forms the romantic interest in this volume and
who is eventually persuaded to read more, and more selectively,
Mifflin draws a parallel between a bookseller and a physician: " 'I
am not a dealer in merchanndise but a specialist in adjusting the
book to the human need. Between ourselves, there is no such thing,
abstractly, as a 'good' book. A book is 'good' only when it meets
some human hunger or refutes some human error. A book that is
good for me would very likely be punk for you. My pleasure is to
prescribe books for such patients as drop in here and are willing to
tell me their symptoms.' "[5] Not surprisingly, many of Mifflin's
"prescriptions" happen to be books that Morley is especially fond of
(and is as busily promoting here as elsewhere). Morley's recommen-
dations include such books as Logan Pearsall Smith's *Trivia*, and, of
course, "classics" to which he hopes to give a wider circulation: the
works of Joseph Conrad, John Keats, and Samuel Butler. In fact, in
the course of the book, Mifflin recommends seventy-eight authors,
several more than once — Stevenson nine times.

Of course, the names of the authors are not just dropped into the
story, but are incorporated into the often excessively discursive tale.
When Roger Mifflin waxes enthusiastic, he is apt to quote from
memory or to reach for a conveniently handy notebook from which
to illustrate his remarks with the words of favorite authors. Morley

uses typographical devices to recommend books to his readers; reproducing a sign which hung in the book shop, he gives Mifflin's prescriptions for "malnutrition of the reading faculty": the list is neatly boxed on a page of *The Haunted Bookshop* under the sign "Rx," and it is over Mifflin's name in boldface type. Later a list of fifteen books is presented, italicized and centered on the page, when Morley ostensibly reproduces the memorandum book notation which one of the characters makes of Mifflin's personal library. A shorter list of seven books is presented when Mifflin consults his shelf of books for reading in bed. Two of Morley's characters, Titania Chapman and Aubrey Gilbert, have literary names, and even the streets in the neighborhood bear the names of authors. To make his point unavoidably clear, Morley arranges the plot in such a way that the key to the mysterious German spy is provided by a code reference to a passage in Carlyle's *Cromwell;*[6] life and literature are intimate, indeed, in *The Haunted Bookshop.*

II Where the Blue Begins

By 1922, Morley felt prepared to attempt his first artistically ambitious book; the result was *Where the Blue Begins*, an artistic success, as well as a popular book, and one that can still be read with pleasure. Written as a dog story, this novel is almost childish in appearance; but it is really an allegory about the human quest for meaning in life. Gissing, a dog named after one of Morley's favorite authors, is the main character; he is a bachelor-dog who lives alone, at the outset, with his butler. In the course of the story Gissing acquires an adopted family, deserts it to explore life, and enters on a search for "where the blue begins." He becomes a department store manager, leaves business for an ill-fated career in the church, spends some time at sea, and finally returns home to resume his familial responsibilities.

Reflecting the domesticity which is so prominent in Morley's poetry of this period, *Where the Blue Begins* suggests that success in the world's eyes does not satisfy all of man's inner needs. By the end of the book, Gissing has rejected the rewards of money and fame and, guided by a newly found religious awe, he is celebrating the joys of family life. The "blue" begins on each individual's own horizon, wherever he may live.

Mr. Gissing does, in fact, have human characteristics: he lives in a house with a dog-butler, "Fuji"; he talks; he walks on his hind legs; and he is a part of a society of similarly humanoid beings. Gissing

received his name through a complicated process: Morley had ac-
quired a terrier puppy some months previous to beginning the book;
and, since he had just purchased a long-desired volume of Gissing's
novels which he had not previously been able to afford, Morley
named the puppy after the novelist; his full name was Haphazard
Gissing I. The puppy immediately became the subject of numerous
Morley essays, and Morley soon began to write a story for his
children that had Gissing as its hero. But, when the story had
reached sufficient length for that original purpose, Morley "could
not," as he said, "end it — it went on and on almost of its own accord."[7] Realizing that it might be preferable to use a purely fictional
name in his story, Morley tried to change it; but he claimed that he
had not been able to do so, however hard he tried.

Morley carried the actual idea for the story around with him "for
over a year, — and then, when it seemed ripe and tender, uncorked
the ink bottle. The thing jumped out with miraculous ease, and ran
off, wagging its tail."[8] Speaking of the way in which the story
evolved in his subconscious before he began writing, Morley wrote
in his diary for January 1, 1922: "*Where the Blue Begins* has been lying fallow in my mind for so long — 'in the fireless cooker,' as
someone has said — that it begins to be savory and tender, like a
simmering stew." The bulk of the actual writing took only six weeks,
"with scarcely any need for revision."[9] After the Morleys had moved
to New York City for the spring of 1922 and were living at the West-
minster Hotel on West 116th Street, Morley wrote *Where the Blue
Begins* at night in a somewhat unorthodox posture. Since "The only
desk available," he later recorded, "was a rickety rosewood toy too
wobbly for decent penmanship," he chose to write while lying on the
floor. Nonetheless, Morley recalled that the story came with such
great ease that, for once, he "did not worry about choice of word or
comfort of posture. Good or bad the fable leaped from the ink and
ran across the paper. That was joy."[10]

When Morley finally completed the book, it caused some conster-
nation among those who were hoping for another *Parnassus*. F. N.
Doubleday, himself, was concerned about the religious implications
of the fable, and Morley later recalled that "Effendi" took him for a
walk in the garden at the Doubleday plant to discuss it. Morley
described the resulting confrontation with humor: Doubleday
"turned upon him in the solitude of the evergreen enclosure and
bade him be explicit. 'The boys say they can't understand a word of
it,' he said. 'Now come clean, what's it all about?' The embarrassed

author said, 'Effendi, I couldn't possibly tell you, out here in the sunshine and at mid-day. But if we could sit down at dusk, by candlelight, or even in the dark, I might be able to give you some idea.' 'Gosh,' said Effendi, 'is it as bad as all that?' "[11]

Morley, however, was genuinely pleased with his work in *Where the Blue Begins;* he confided to a friend, "My God, I really think it's rather a beautiful book. I wonder who wrote it? I'll tell you a secret. I love the damn book."[12] His readers' reactions were, however, more ambiguous. Charles Puckette of Doubleday thought the book blasphemous.[13] Even Morley's mother was disturbed by some of the ideas developed in the novel. She wrote to him on August 3, 1922, that "what pains me and what I think will shock in 'the Blue' is the familiarity with which certain Sacred (to many) subjects are treated. . . . What I personally most dislike is the description of God as a dog 'with shining jowls' and of Gissing's recognition of the filthy tramp for God." Attempting on August 11, 1922, to answer her criticism, Morley wrote to his mother that "The whole thing is at any rate intended as a powerful pro-religion fable, not at all cynical (in the literal sense of cynical! viz. *doggish!)* atheism. Perhaps it is intended to convey — very gingerly — that there may be a whole realm of law and emotion and being as greatly superior to our clay as our own is to the honorable and pathetic world of dogs." The scene of which Morley's mother spoke — the scene toward which Morley claimed he had written the whole story — also bothered another Doubleday editor, Lyman Beecher Stowe, who wrote to the author asking him to omit the recognition scene; convinced of its importance, Morley refused. Nonetheless, readers in general enjoyed the book partly as a satire directed against the prominent Episcopal bishop, William T. Manning, in the character of "Bishop Borzoi."

The novel ranges from pure fantasy to piercing irreverence, with frequent philosophical digressions. Gissing, wondering to himself whether children are worth the effort required to raise them, muses that "No one who is not a parent realizes, for example, the extraordinary amount of buttoning and unbuttoning necessary in rearing children. I calculate that 50,000 buttonings are required for each one before it reaches the age of even rudimentary independence. With the energy so expended one might write a great novel or chisel a statue. Never mind: these urchins must be my Works of Art. If one were writing a novel, he could not delegate to a hired servant the composition of laborious chapters."[14] As the father of four children, Morley evidently spoke with autobiographical intent; the parallel in his attitudes toward writing a novel and rearing a child is striking, but it is typical of Morley's beliefs about the identity of literature and life. As we might expect, Gissing does begin writing a book late in the novel; he has problems when the puppies destroy his typewriter — another reminder of Morley's own home life?

But this is not an explicitly literary novel: it is more nearly autobiographical, with the suburban setting (in Canine Estates), the children, and even an Atlantic cruise, Morley's favorite recreation. There is a tribute to New York City that lies halfway between a travelogue essay and a poem: "There is a city so proud, so mad, so beautiful and young, that even heaven has retreated, lest her placid purity be too nearly tempted by that brave tragic spell."[15]

Although *Where the Blue Begins* was also published in a large-print, illustrated, children's edition in 1924, it is a profoundly and successfully serious book which illustrates the problems that were beginning to occupy Morley's more serious thoughts. The measure of its popular success can, perhaps, be suggested by the fact that it had sold over twenty-five thousand copies by 1937. It is not difficult to see why, soon after completing *Where the Blue Begins*, Morley announced that, "I regard it as my First Book."[16]

III   Thunder on the Left

Thunder on the Left, published in 1925, created a sensation in the literary worlds of England and America. In Morley's autobiographical *John Mistletoe* (226), he records a conversation that he had with "one of the greatest and boldest of living writers" concerning a book he had written. The unidentified author exclaimed, "What a fool you were to write that book; *what* a fool! How you will regret it presently. Thank God I always had sense enough not to try to write about the insides of things. Why did you do it?" When Mistletoe-Morley answered, "I had to," the other replied, "Was it laid upon you? It was. Don't attempt to deny it! — Then I understand perfectly."[17] Although most readers easily identified Morley as "Mistletoe," probably few of them realized either the identity of the famous author, or the title of the book being discussed. Morley revealed both facts in an article entitled "A Collaboration Without Reproach or Regret," which appeared in *The New York Times* of November 5, 1933, and again in his introductory essay to *Letters of Rudyard Kipling*, issued by Thomas B. Mosher in 1936. Morley there revealed that the remarks were made to him by Kipling about *Thunder on the Left* on the morning of June 15, 1926, which the two writers spent together in London. After first appearing in serial form in *Harper's Magazine*, the novel was issued by Doubleday, Page in November, 1925; before going out of print ten years later, *Thunder on the Left* had sold over eighty-two-thousand copies in America.

The novel, a fantasy, opens at a birthday party that is attended by a group of children. They begin to wonder aloud whether they really want to grow up — are their parents genuinely happy, and would they tell them if they were not? Ten-year-old Martin is magically enabled to spy on the affairs of the adults, to try to determine whether it is worthwhile for the children to become like them. When the scene and time suddenly shift, all the children except Martin have become adults. In their adult roles, they are planning a weekend picnic when, unexpectedly, Martin, physically a man but still a child in thoughts and actions, appears as an unrecognized and uninvited guest. Sensing the unhappiness and frustrations of his hosts' lives, Martin witnesses a tragic panorama of events that involve marital infidelity and that result from the inability of people to communicate effectively with each other. The ghost of his sister, who had died in childhood, appears and warns him to leave. Unwilling to do so, Martin only escapes back to the world of his childhood at the cost of the lives of the three children of his hosts, who are abruptly killed when a loose balcony railing gives way. A final chapter returns to the birthday party, where it is made clear that even Martin will have to grow up, like the rest.

That next-to-last fatal scene brought Morley much criticism, since the author had not fully prepared his readers for such an inexplicable tragedy. Frank Morley, himself an experienced writer and editor, wrote to his brothers Christopher and Felix that "the catastrophe there was just plain unintelligible" (April 19, 1949). In an attempt to explain the scene, Christopher Morley did give his rationale years later: "It is cruel and was intended to be cruel. . . . Of course it must end in destruction of the innocent children because all innocence must atone for the guilty, only on these terms can life exist."[18]

One of Martin's hosts, George, who is really Martin grown up, is a professional publicist who is engaged in composing advertising booklets for a summer resort. His ineffectual efforts to write give rise to some Morleyesque musings about the proper conditions for creative work: "His mind was too agitated to compose, but he began clattering a little on the machine, at random, just to give the impression that he was working. Why should anyone invent a 'noiseless' typewriter, he wondered? The charm of a typewriter was that it *did* make a noise, a noise that shut out the racket other people were making. What a senseless idea, to imagine that he could really get some work done here, buried in the country. He could not concentrate because there was nothing to concentrate *from*."[19]

George's wife, Phyllis, commits some literary speculations while sitting in her bath and thinking about Shakespeare; according to narrator Morley, "Now, in an intimate understanding that many an erudite scholar has never attained, she perceived what the man with a beard was driving at. The plays, which she had always politely respected as well-bred women do respect serious institutions, were something more than gusts of fantastic tinsel interspersed with foul jokes — jokes she knew were foul without understanding them. They were parables of the High Cost of Living — the cost to brain and heart and spirit of this wildly embarrasing barter called life."[20]

It was, as *Parnassus on Wheels* demonstrated, one of Morley's recurrent themes that literature, especially "great" literature, speaks to the needs and emotions of real, average people; and the characters of *Thunder on the Left* are designed to bear out Morley's thesis. Morley even includes a defense of George's — and, by implication, his own — publicity work, when George, sitting down at his desk,

. . . felt a rational pride in this composition. It was in the genially fulsome vein esteemed by railroad companies. Even if people weren't tranquil, in a place so competently described, they ought to be. He thought there was a neatness in that touch about Dark Harbour and its bright future. Phyllis was probably right when she often said it was a shame Mr. Granville should spend his talents in mere publicity work when he might so easily write something famous — fiction, for instance. These are my fictions, he always replied, pointing to his private shelf of advertising pamphlets, neatly bound and gilded as his Works.[21]

Fictions, as George proposed, are more than imitations of reality: they are also statements about the potential of life, which can transform life through their impact. Thus George's advertising and the novels he might have written both fall under the same fictional heading, for each speaks not merely of life as it is but as it might be.

Morley first seems to have thought of the general idea behind *Thunder on the Left* in 1920; he wrote in his journal on March 13 of that year: "Today an idea came to me of writing either a story or a little play about a small boy turned into an adult, bodily, yet retaining his child's mind, his simplicity, candor & poetic imagination. The beginning would be a number of children discussing their elders, and arguing as to the desirability of growing up." However, having written a few pages, Morley reported that he "saw at once that the thing was beyond me. I had to wait till I could grow up to it. When we got to France in June, 1924, I tackled it."[22]

Perhaps because he had considered the possibility of writing *Thunder on the Left* in play form, Morley was especially conscious of the importance of the setting: the action is centered around an estate, on an island, which has been vacant for many years before being rented for that summer. He experimented with the subject in a short story, "Continuity," which was written sometime before November, 1921. In that story, two men spend the night in a lonely, deserted house; one of them wakes during the night to see a ghostlike apparition: a young child on a tricycle, exploring the grounds by midnight. The next morning he learns that the former tenants had a young son and that they moved out shortly after he was killed in an accident.

Morley's style in *Thunder on the Left* shows the beginnings of an epigrammatical tendency which was to make much of his later work eminently quotable. Typical phrases are: "Life is a foreign language: all men mispronounce it;" "arguments are like cats: if you take them up by the tail they twist and scratch you;" and "even thinking about God is no excuse for keeping others out of the bathroom."

Sensing that an indirect approach might most successfully communicate his theme, Morley presented his ideas in the form of a fantasy. His feelings about this genre were expressed in a 1925 review of novels by Elinor Wylie and Stella Benson; at that time, Morley wrote that "there are always excellent reasons for silence. One worthy reason is that you have nothing to say. Another is that what you are thinking is too important to be said, or would become untrue if uttered. The recourse of those who feel they have something to say, but desire to avoid the bitterness of being understood, has been (ever since AEsop) the fable or fantasy."[23] These comments apply with special force to *Thunder on the Left,* which raises real questions in our minds about the virtues of "growing up," as well as about the frequent lack of honesty in our attitudes and behavior toward our children.

In the same review Morley mentioned a theory that he held about fantasy, expressed by the words "the importance of any fable can be gauged by the area of silence it covers." Developing his theory in a later essay, Morley spoke of "one neglected consideration in the art of writing . . . Not how much can you do *for* the reader, but how much can you cajole him into doing for you. How much of your book can the reader write for you, in his own mind? I coined an aphorism once — coined is too precise a word; I mean I laboriously chopped it out — that one test of any form of expression is the area of silence it covers."[24] Believing that the less he needed to write, the greater would be the ultimate impact upon his readers, Morley worked to keep *Thunder on the Left* relatively unfurnished. For the relative complexity of its plot and theme, it became a remarkably short and compact work, about sixty-eight-thousand words in length.

Most striking is the atmosphere established in the novel. The tense, electric expectation of a summer storm on the island and the crickets chattering in the bushes contribute to the feeling of suspense. And the combination of broad humor in George's relationship with his wife and the stark tragedy of the children's deaths sharpens the irony of the plot; some of the chapter endings are breathlessly exciting. The characters poignantly attempt to express their emotions to each other: " 'George.' She intended to say, 'I love you.' But of their own accord the words changed themselves before they escaped into voice. 'George, do you love me?' " Suffused in literature and human drama, *Thunder on the Left* illustrates the problems of children trying to come to terms with adulthood, while the adults around them struggle to make sense of their own lives. It remains one of Morley's most readable and satisfying novels.

IV   Human Being

Thunder on the Left was to be Christopher Morley's last interesting novel for seven years. In the meantime, he published a trivial foreign-policy spoof called *Pleased to Meet You*, and a new version of Charles M. Barras's play, *The Black Crook*, which Morley had produced in his Hoboken theater venture; retitled *Rudolph and Amina* and recast as a novel, the book is replete with references to imaginary stage directions and is written in fairy-tale style. *John Mistletoe*, published in 1930, is entirely autobiographical, containing detailed information about Christopher Morley's childhood in Haverford, as well as numerous essays, poems, and anecdotal stories from his past. Written near his fortieth birthday, *John Mistletoe* is significant largely as a break between Morley's younger, lighter works and the more ambitious novels that were to follow. While the young Christopher Morley was often described (to his annoyance) as "whimsical," from 1930 until his death fewer traces of this quality can be discerned in his novels.

Christopher Morley's unique viewpoint about the complicated business of ordinary living is developed more sharply in his novel, *Human Being*, than anywhere else in his works. A warm, humorous book, its goal is "To catch a human being in the very act of being human, and to set it down without chemical preservatives."[25] Composed in installments for his *Saturday Review* columns, *Human Being* is full of the things Morley loved best, from the statue of Diana to a theater episode. The plot is based on the efforts of Lawrence Hubbard, retired accountant for a publishing firm, to construct a biography of Richard Roe, a former employee of the firm who had died some months before. In the course of his investigations, Hubbard uncovers several remarkable events in Roe's life that illustrate the rich complexity hidden in an apparently "ordinary" man. More importantly, Hubbard becomes personally entangled with many of the people Roe had been involved with, especially his former secretary and mistress, Minnie Hutzler, with whom Hubbard himself finally falls in love. As Morley describes the book, "This is not only the biography of Richard Roe but a biography of that biography."[26]

Morley evolved the idea for *Human Being* over a very long period of time; the first mention appears in a list of planned books in his journal of March 2, 1920: ". . . stories revolving about the character of one man, who never appears, but is the motif of the whole, showing his personality from different angles, and leaving the reader to make up his mind as to his man's nature — one characteristic touch, brought out in all the episodes, will perhaps explain apparent contradictions." By 1926, his concept had evolved nearly to the final plan used in *Human Being;* his journal for March 2 recorded: "*John Doe* would be the title for a Tom Joneslike novel of American life, the hero to be a traveling salesman — perhaps for a religious publishing house? . . . . A long book, full of the egregious humors of American life; a very plain and unembroidered book; to be written, as I once said to myself, 'like a translation from the Russian,' so that none of its merit would depend on mere 'style' or verbal charm; but lucid; strongly *narrative;* a merry, droll, candid book, with its deeper pathos well concealed. A book *humorous* in the true sense."

One of the important details in *Human Being* was Richard Roe's "Iron Ration," the small package of essentials that he finally took with him when, just before his death, he decided to leave his home and business. The origins of the Iron Ration appear in Morley's journal for December 6, 1926: "There was a man once who kept in a rolltop desk a little package wrapped in newspaper — a clean shirt, a pair of pyjamas, a change of underwear, a handkerchief, a clean collar, a pair of socks. This, though never used, was his Iron Ration — at any moment he cd [sic] seize it and flee away on a train if life got too hard."

Having long felt New York's power and mystery and convinced of the importance of the average man's unsung existence, Morley got the idea for the actual story line of *Human Being*, as he later told an interviewer, "when I read an obit about a man dying of heart failure on the Hoboken ferry. And I began to think about the middle-class man, the inarticulate and frustrated little man. Then I began to think about the people who might have known him, and of some of them talking about him and it was as though I were sitting in a dark theatre, with the characters coming out onto the stage."[27]

The details of daily life in New York permeate *Human Being*. Morley frequently converted what he had actually experienced into fiction, with the aid of notes taken on the spot. Jules's tiny, intimate restaurant, so convincingly described in the novel, was patterned after Christ Cella's place on East 45th Street where Morley's "Three Hours for Lunch Club" used to meet. Morley's memorandum book shows that his friend Oliver Perry once said, when Cella was persuaded to perform for the group, "Life seems so simple when you hear the accordian"; these words are attributed to one of the characters in *Human Being*, Gene Vogelsang. A Doubleday salesman, Frank C. Henry, once had to sleep on a mattress spread on top of a grand piano while on the road, because, according to Morley's notes, a convention had preempted the hotel; in the novel, Richard Roe is allowed that unusual experience. And the small fire that leads to Richard Roe's invention of a non-flammable penholder is patterned after a fire that was accidentally started by Morley himself in a bookstore in Nashville, Tennessee.

Other details were sharpened by field excursions that Morley often liked to take. To be better able to describe Richard Roe's office in the Flatiron Building, Morley interviewed the renting agent for that building, under the pretense of planning to lease an office there. The small, unglamorous sides of New York life which Morley loved, like the Diana statue and the Sixth Avenue El, frequently appear as Richard Roe's own perceptions; and they sometimes lead to excessively long digressions about the joys of life in New York.

Morley thought of *Human Being* as "an interesting experiment in backward narrative," and he also felt that "it might be esteemed by

literary people as an interesting *tour de force*. . . ."[28] He noted that
the book was planned "exactly as a modern New York building is
planned, with setbacks — successive terraces of vista to give more
sunlight to the reader and to throw more light upon the life and
times of Richard Roe." However, many of the "setbacks" are in-
trusive, and the transitions can be dislocating by their great number.
The structure itself sometimes seems to bulge, partly because
Morley tried to cover so much material in one volume: the subjects
jump from apartment life to office routine to the life of salesmen on
the road; the scene shifts from New York City to Detroit to Boston
and to Washington — and frequent stopovers along the way are included.

Further complicating the novel is the multiplicity of narrative
points of view; sometimes the story is being told by Hubbard, the
biographer; sometimes by the omniscient author; and occasionally
by Morley, apparently, as a character in the book. Morley noted the
problems this complexity might cause early in the novel by remarking that "I can't always be bothered to put in careful quotation-
marks in the exact places. Quotation-marks try to imply that some
definite person made some particular remark. But almost everybody
says everything if you give them a chance." Although most of the
chapters are divided by a skipped line into sections, that typographical device is sometimes omitted between changes in point of view.
For example, on one occasion Hubbard shows up for a drink and
chat with the author, but his own thoughts are revealed not in the
course of the conversation but by the narrator. Frequently Hubbard's name is invoked as responsible for words apparently Morley's
own; in fact, as Morley admitted years later, "I am not quite sure
whether Hubbard is sufficiently differentiated from Richard Roe. As
I look at Hubbard from now he is a little too much like John Doe."[29]
While Morley recognized the confusion, he failed to pinpoint it:
Hubbard is not so much like John Doe as he is like Morley himself.

The cast of characters is, for Morley, Dickensian in number, but
one of them has a special clarity and reality. As Morley put it, "one
of those miracles happened that, in a writer's secret heart, justify
everything: the unexpected emergence of a Character who gets up
and moves things around by unpremeditated vitality. Minnie
Hutzler just walked in and took charge."[30] The dark woman of the
novel, a Jewess full of courage and encouragement for Richard Roe,
she develops into a memorable and believable character, rivaling
Manhattan as the heroine of the novel.

Human Being is filled with the publishing industry which Morley knew and loved so well: for most of his career Richard Roe worked as a travelling book salesman for a firm with many non-accidental resemblances to Doubleday, Page and Company. Morley incudes a number of comments that reflect his belief in the importance of literature to life. For example, a group of businessmen at lunch — many associated with the publishing industry but none of them writers — listens attentively to an excerpt from a recent novel which one of them has clipped; Morley notes: "The clippings and memorabilia which hardheaded citizens carry in their wallets are often important."[31]

Morley attributes to the "Erskine Brothers" publishing house the Doubleday principle which he had made his own: "they regarded publishing definitely as a business, not as a branch of culture."[32] When Richard Roe, conscientiously selling books, decides to read some of them, he finds to his surprise that ". . . the mystic art of reading, a much rarer gift than might be supposed, was not natural to him. He could never accomplish it except when free from all distraction. He was instinctively alert in all personal relationships, but print was a foreign unreal medium in which he proceeded with difficulty. He was embarrassed by a native respectfulness toward books, a feeling that they are to be taken seriously."[33] The inner conflicts of a man making his living peddling a product that he respects but really doesn't understand add dimension to the shy character Morley and Hubbard are trying to portray. Several chapters are devoted to actual episodes of bookselling on the road, and they reveal a rather sardonic attitude toward the purchasing methods of bookstores.

Several extensive references to the theater underscore the fact that Morley wrote *Human Being* just at the conclusion of his Hoboken experiment. He quite shamelessly praises his own production of *The Black Crook*, as well as his *Troilus and Cressida* revision which he titled *The Trojan Horse* and which appeared both as a novel and a play. Late in the book a flashback recalls Morley's own firsthand involvement in the business end of theater — in fact, a crucial episode revolves around the embezzlement of box-office monies by Roe's brother, probably a reference to the unfortunate end of the Hoboken adventure.

Hubbard never finishes his biography of Richard Roe, remarking "I don't regret the time and struggle I've put in on it. Maybe it's taught me a little more kindness. Kindness is no mood for a modern biographer."[34] What Morley seems to be saying in *Human Being* is that biographers neglect the most fascinating subjects available, the rich complexities of every human being, sympathetically and carefully examined. Despite the technical complexities of the novel, *Human Being* succeeds in conveying that message clearly and convincingly.

V The Trojan Horse

The love of Troilus, one of the heroes of the Trojan War, for the beautiful Cressida, who proved false, is an old story which first appeared in the apparently fourth-century work of the pseudonymous "Dictys of Crete." Important versions of the tale since that first effort include Boccaccio's *Il Filostrato*, Chaucer's *Troilus and Criseyde*, a sixth-century narrative of the fall of Troy ascribed to Dares the Phrygian, and Shakespeare's *Troilus and Cressida*. Shakespeare borrowed from Chaucer the story of the lovers, but Morley felt that, in so doing, he had "hardened and toughened and cynicized" the legend, and "had lost all Chaucer's adorable crystalline naiveté and candor."[35] The *Trojan Horse*, Morley's modernized version of the legend, is an attempt to present the love story in such a way as to preserve the beauty of Chaucer's original conception while also introducing many new elements: the result is an entirely new treatment.

Morley has added some completely new and contemporary characters to the drama: Fuscus, a Negro servant through whose admiring eyes Troilus is described; Ilium, the Radio Voice of Troy, a reporter of political happenings; Dictes, Pandarus's English butler; and Sarpedoni (based on Chaucer's King Sarpedon), proprietor of a Shore Dinner roadhouse to which the Trojans and Greeks repair for entertainment. Other characters, mentioned briefly in Chaucer, become more important figures in Morley's version. For example, King Priam presides over the dinner table before which troop his fifty sons; Queen Hecuba, Dormouse-like, constantly sits nodding on her throne; and Cassandra, the voice of Doom, is never heeded but always proves to have been correctly informed.

The setting is purportedly that of ancient Troy, but, "as we look carefully, it's odd: among medieval walls and classic temples we see perpendicular modern skyscrapers, radio towers, filling stations, and a seaside roadhouse. . . ." The modern setting is not a superfluous gesture; in addition to bringing the ancient legend up to date, Morley hoped to point out, through the voice of Cassandra, the parallels between the Fall of Troy and the dangers facing contem-

porary civilization in the rise of Fascism and Nazism in 1937. Troy,
Morley insisted, was "our own," and Cassandra was warning
modern Americans when she declared ironically,

> Civilization, roll your one good ear
> Deep in the goosedown pillow:
> Go to sleep!

When he dramatized his novel in 1941, Morley called the play "A
Bed-time Story," comparing the Fall of Troy to the Fall of Warsaw
in 1939.

If *The Trojan Horse* did nothing more than inspire a reading of
Chaucer's work, it would very likely have succeeded in Morley's
eyes; his love for the poet of Middle English shows clearly in his
dedication: "To G.C./Come Back And All Will Be Forgiven." Much
shorter than Chaucer's work, *The Trojan Horse* is also atypical
Morley, because of its few digressions or literary lectures.
Nonetheless, Morley continued in this unusual novel his practice of
emphasizing the proximity of literature to life by interspersing blank
verse and lyrical poetry with his prose. Included in these are
"Dichotomy" and "A Song For Eros," two excellent poems that
humorously examine the nature of love.

Perhaps the sparest in style of all of Morley's novels, *The Trojan
Horse* was written during a period when its author was aware of
current interest in streamlining. Under the influence of his friend
Buckminster Fuller, Morley became intrigued with the possibilities
of streamlining his own literary creations. In 1935, after riding with
Fuller in his efficiently designed Dymaxion car, Morley wrote "I'm
interested in this not just as a car, which is relatively unimportant,
but as a symbol of what is forward in every phase of living. Not only
in locomotion, architecture, shipbuilding, but in morals and
manners, clothes, religions, even in literature we grope for the
Streamline: to reduce unnecessary wind resistance."[36]

Speaking over the radio in December of that year, Morley ap-
proved of Virginia Woolf's statement that "the novelist of the future
will take reality for granted." He commented on that line in detail:
"By that I suppose he won't waste time and energy on describing
details of furniture or scenery that the reader can well supply —
would even prefer to supply — from his own mind."[37] In that talk
Morley also mentioned Willa Cather's essay, "The Novel
Démeublé," which he had included in his *Modern Essays of 1924*.

The first line of Cather's essay states the theme: "The novel for a long while, has been over-furnished." Almost echoing Woolf and Cather, Morley commented on *The Trojan Horse* following its completion in these words: "I have most positively tried to omit all merely fatty or connective tissue; all irrelevant describings and furnishings; leaving it to the collaborative reader to create it in his own image. . . . Only so, I think, can we suggest that the most modern joys and puzzles and emotions are also ancient, also personal."[38]

The meeting of the lovers, for example, is effected swiftly in Morley's version of the story: Troilus sees Cressida for the first time and falls in love with her; Pandarus shows Cressida some youthful love poems and leads her to the balcony as Troilus rides by (an adaptation of a Shakespearean detail). Cressida, in her turn, is attracted and deeply moved; a dinner party is arranged; and Troilus and Cressida are left together. In Chaucer's treatment, on the other hand, Troilus falls in love off-stage before the poem begins; Pandarus intercedes and learns of Cressida's willingness to be served by Troilus as a respectful knight; she then sees Troilus by chance but does not immediately fall in love. There is an exchange of letters before the blushing heroine is vouchsafed another sight of Troilus; they meet for romance only after an elaborate scheme of devices is put into operation. Morley's tempo is, therefore, noticeably brisker and more "modern."

Morley intelligently adapts some of Chaucer's devices, such as the rainstorm used to bring the lovers together. Where Chaucer was ambiguous in his explanation of the cause of the storm, Morley clearly makes it an example of *deus ex machina* (" 'It was ordained,' says Cassandra serenely."). A more significant change appears in Morley's use of the brooch that alerts Troilus to Cressida's unfaithfulness. Rather than simply announcing, as Chaucer does, that Troilus discovers "a brooch that he Criseyde gave that morrow" pinned to Diomedes' surcoat, Morley prepares the way for that discovery by showing Troilus giving Cressida the ornament as she leaves for the Greek camp. The brooch — actually Troilus's squadron pin — is described in detail as "a little ornament in gold and blue enamel." Thus the significance of Troilus's discovery is immediately clear as he makes it; the author need not interrupt to explain it.

In Morley's tale the love story is made more palatable to the modern reader by making Troilus a sympathetic figure; he is strong enough to bend a bronze into a circle when angry, but he is also capable of writing love poetry to Cressida. Chaucer's less appealing hero is prone to sob, sigh, and swoon. Similarly, Morley's Cressida is an active, decisive woman, equally capable of dignity and surrender; Chaucer's Criseyde is more apt to blush, to procrastinate, and to discuss matters with herself at great length.

Morley also gives the affair a realistic touch, for Troilus notes that his love's eyebrows "crunch like bacon." A psychological aspect of their love is revealed when Morley's Cressida tells Troilus that "I didn't *want* to meet you," and when she makes him cry aloud with her declaration "My beautiful, my beautiful, must I know you? — Why can't I just have you to myself, in dreams?" These sentiments reflect a comment Morley had made in 1923 about poets: "They know the meaning of that old Latin phrase *Desiderio pulchriora:* things are more beautiful when we yearn for them: and indeed the man (whoever he was) who first wrote those words is more present to my spirit than many I see daily in my affairs."[39]

The love of Troilus and Cressida gains an added dimension from the contrasting character of Pandarus, who brings the young people together. Morley's go-between develops a positive personality of his own, for he never sinks to the depths of Shakespeare's Pandarus, nor does he find it necessary, like Chaucer's character, to frequently deny that he is a bawd. Morley's man is a subtle blend of cynic and vulnerable human being; when, upon learning of her unfaithfulness, he curses the niece whom he has loved, he is easy to empathize with.

Morley also alters the ending of the story. Following orthodox Christian teaching, Chaucer closes his poem with a vision of Troilus in heaven. He looks down to earth, laughs to himself at the grief of those who wept for him, but damns all those who are not seeking after religious piety. With a touch of irony, Morley describes Troilus and Diomedes, who betrayed him, exercising together in the Elysian Fields, "in endless laughter, angers forgotten"; they simply do not notice the newcomer, the unnamed Cressida. She concludes the novel with the comment, "Who were those boys . . . There was something familiar about them?"

The Trojan Horse also appeared in a full-length dramatic version by Morley in 1941, published by Random House. Morley began work on the play in September, 1939, and finished it two months later. After some revision it was produced at the Millpond Playhouse in Roslyn; the run lasted sixty performances, beginning October 30, 1940. Although such notables as Sherwood Anderson and Dorothy

Thompson were among the audience, only the opening night drew much of a crowd. The play's failure may well have been due to the production and locale, but a similar lack of public response had also dogged *The Trojan Horse* as a novel. Morley seems to have done a competent job of dramatizing his work; the lines read well, and they lend themselves easily to stage presentation. Both as novel and play, *The Trojan Horse* provided a chance for Christopher Morley to experiment with new and different styles and literary forms. While he found the opportunities rewarding, and consequently felt much affection for his work, neither the novel nor the drama represents a major contribution to the Morley canon.

VI Kitty Foyle

More people read *Kitty Foyle* than any other work that Christopher Morley wrote. It became a national best seller, it was made into an Academy-Award-winning movie, and it even came out in a paperback edition. It is almost surprising, therefore, to discover that *Kitty Foyle* is among the best books Morley published: it is neither Morley turned sensationalist nor watered down for general consumption, but Christopher Morley at the peak of his wit and style.

Written as a kind of interior monologue, the story is told by Kitty Foyle, a working-class girl from Philadelphia. With frequent jumps in time, both forward and backward, she narrates events stretching from her early childhood to her late twenties; she thereby covers the years from World War I through the Great Depression. The central plot, however, revolves around Kitty's affair with Wyn Strafford, a young scion of the Philadelphia Main Line. When Kitty becomes pregnant, she decides not to tell Wyn; instead, she resorts to an abortion rather than permit his family to force him into a marriage that would have torn him away from his family and his natural environment. Wyn soon after marries a socially acceptable girl, and Kitty becomes a career woman in New York and Chicago. As the novel ends, Kitty has become involved with a Jewish doctor, Mark Eisen; her feelings about him are less passionate than they were for Wyn, and she is still in the process of reconciling herself to that fact.

Kitty is neither particularly intellectual nor especially literary, and her relative uninvolvement with books makes her an atypical Morley protagonist. In fact, the absence of much literary sermonizing might help account for the unusual success of the novel. The narration is often quite lyrical, even poetic. Fragments of poems which Morley published during the late 1930's appear in the text; one example appears late in the novel, when Kitty thinks to herself, "But when you're putting on an act how you love to be caught up on it. By the right person, that is."[40] This comment matches neatly with these lines from Morley's "Two Sonnets To Themselves":

> You like to laugh? Sure, I can make you laugh,
> And, if you wished it, I could make you cry.
> You like to put an act on, and get half
> Way through, and be caught up with? So do I.[41]

Kitty Foyle does develop one period of serious literary activity when Wyn hires Kitty to help him start "Philly" Magazine, a local version of *The New Yorker*. While the episode advances their fledgling romance, the magazine fails ingloriously due to the combined incompetence of the amateur staff and the arrival of the market crash.

Although the novel was written in 1938, Morley had thought of the basic idea as early as 1921. In one of his old *New York Evening Post* columns called "Thoughts in the Subway," Morley had written of the new generation of young women who worked as stenographers and typists in the city. In that column he had observed that "they are a new generation of their sex, cool, assured, even capable. They are happy, because they are so perishable, because (despite their naive assumption of certainty) one knows them so delightfully only as an innocent ornament of this business world of which they are so ignorant." Empathizing with these young career girls, Morley expressed his conviction of their importance by focusing on them in another essay, "A Call for the Author": "A girl, slender, gayly unconscious of admiration, poises on one foot at the edge of the subway platform, leaning over to see if the train is coming." This sort of girl, symbolizing the new wave of social development in the city, was to become Kitty Foyle.

It is clear from Morley's notes that Kitty was not patterned after any one girl of his acquaintance, as many readers assumed. Morley's interest in young career girls, after germinating in the 1921 essay, grew during his close contact with many of them after 1924 in the offices of *The Saturday Review of Literature*, where he had been assigned secretaries of his own. However, he did not have a "private" secretary until after the publication of *Kitty Foyle*, when he set up an office of his own and depended upon the assistance of Elizabeth Winspear.

The girls of *The Saturday Review* office were the same sort of good-natured girls with a tendency toward wise-cracks that Kitty and her friends were to become. The office girls had been nicknamed "The Mermaids" after a nautical advertisement for subscriptions which appeared in the magazine, and Morley referred to them by this term in his notes. One such record recounts the story of the Mermaid who finally decided to marry a man of less-than-ideal qualities because she badly wanted to have a child. She planned — or so she told the office — to inform her husband after their baby was born, "Your subscription expires with this issue." Morley also met many young career girls in department stores and bookshops as he conducted his many lecture tours around the country; he knew particularly well many salesmen and saleswomen in Chicago.

Morley, however, did not depend entirely on his personal experiences with career girls. He conducted interviews on at least three separate occasions with career women from Germaine Monteil and from Luzier's to learn about the dynamics of the cosmetics industry in which Kitty was to work. Kitty, therefore, is an entirely invented character, made up from Morley's memory, research, and imagination. As Morley himself wrote elsewhere, "So far as I know, Kitty Foyle had no individual model, though several sources."[42] On a later occasion he remarked, "I have often said to myself, 'She is not my type:' I mean, I do not believe I myself would find her tempting or even amusing because I would not be likely to penetrate her armor of reserve (which is considerable). This may seem absurd, since she has no existence except in my own mind."[43]

It is probably unrewarding, then, to search for the "original" of Kitty Foyle. What is significant about Kitty is her sociological meaning. The author of *The Stereotype of the Single Woman in American Novels* understood what Morley was trying to portray in the character of Kitty: "She will be remembered for making articulate, with remarkable insight and courage and in a colorful vernacular, what thousands of girls, by 1940, had experienced, observed, or imagined."[44]

More than any other Christopher Morley publication, *Kitty Foyle* not only created, as we have noted, a stir of national and even international proportions but was banned in both Ireland and Italy as a result of Catholic reaction to the abortion episode. An official publication of the Episcopal Church in Pennsylvania, *The Church News*, editorialized against it as "obscene literature," and even some booksellers who were old friends of the author, like Marcella Hahner of Chicago's Marshall Field, were upset by the book. Particularly disturbed were some Philadelphia Main Liners; Wanamaker's department store sold it only by request, and then from under the counter; many Pennsylvania Quakers (and Morley's father had been a Friend) objected, as demonstrated by this letter, written to Morley on a delicate sheet of blue stationery:

> Shadowild,
> Strafford, Pennsylvania
>
> Dear Christopher Morley,
>   I wish thee had not written *Kitty Foyle*.
>
> Sincerely,
> Martha Serene Lewis

The citizens of Conshohocken were also aroused because the name of their town had been used in the book as a curse word by Kitty's father. The president of Morley's alma mater, Haverford College, W. W. Comfort, disliked the book; even the publisher, J. W. Lippincott, had his doubts. Morley tried to reassure him by writing that "that vulgarity is not — as you charmingly and innocently suggested — lugged in on purpose, either to scandalize or to amuse. It *has* to be there. Believe me, it causes me as much anxiety as it possibly could you; it is going to offend a great many people, some of whom are near and dear to myself; it is going to cause surprise or shock or annoyance to a good many critics. . . ."[45]

Some of Morley's friends assumed that *Kitty Foyle* had been written solely to make a lot of money. Particularly stunned by the novel, Morley's friend and fellow author, T. A. Daly, told a reporter, "He jumped into that field for one reason — to make money."[46] Another close friend, Philip S. Clarke, wrote to Morley: ". . . in the spirit of candor that always prevails between us, I must say that it isn't the best thing you ever did. A man with your genius doesn't need to fall back on an out-house and an abortion except as a relaxation from valuable production. I know it paid, and I'm glad of it. Serves 'em damned well right. But don't do it again unless you have to." Clarke seems to have forgotten that, when Morley had been in serious financial straits in 1930, he had shown no inclination to solve his difficulties by prostituting his talents. Morley had other ways of supplementing his income than vulgarizing the novels he cared about so much: in 1938 he wrote, anonymously, a series of advertisements for the Schlitz Brewing Company, employing his flair for promotional writing with considerable craftsmanship.

In fact, *Kitty Foyle* was assisted by an intelligent advertising campaign that was based on copy supplied by the author. Henry R. Luce praised the campaign as "the most provocative advertising of any kind that I have ever seen," and The Publisher's Ad Club awarded an honorable mention to Lippincott's advertising manager for the effort, deeming it the best advertising campaign during the last half of 1939. As the fruit of these labors, *Kitty Foyle* became the nation's number two seller for 1940; was translated into five languages; and became in succession, a movie, a play, and a radio soap opera.

Morley did feel strongly about *Kitty Foyle*, and he never deprecated the book in later remarks. In the late 1930's Morley felt that he needed to speak for the thousands of White Collar Girls who seemed to him as worthy of attention as the poor farmers that John Steinbeck had described in *The Grapes of Wrath*, which had appeared in 1939, at the same time as *Kitty Foyle;* in fact, Morley called the career girls "sharecroppers in the Dust Bowl of business." As Morley told a reporter interviewing him about *Kitty Foyle,* "Joseph Conrad once told me, 'How thrilling it is when mutes find a voice!' Here is a whole flotilla of marvelous creatures without a voice."[47]

One of the purposes of *Kitty Foyle* was established in the dedicatory motto that appeared after the title page — one taken from George Saintsbury's *The English Novel:* "All the requirements of the novelist are subsidiary to this, that he shall in his pages show us the result of the workings of the heart, and brain, of the body, soul, and spirit of actual or possible human beings." To emphasize this desire to focus on characterization in the novel, Morley wrote copy for an advertisement in which, under the heading, "A Jury of Her Peers," Kitty Foyle appeared as the most recent fictional female in a series which ran from Daniel Defoe's Moll Flanders through Nathaniel Hawthorne's Hester Prynne, Charlotte Bronte's Jane Eyre, and W. M. Thackeray's Becky Sharp. Morley felt that he had succeeded in his aim; he later wrote to a correspondent that this novel "seems to me my most substantial contribution in the way of character portrayal."[48]

Another indication of the respect Morley felt for his creation was that he considered publishing the book anonymously, feeling that it was Kitty's book; he realized that it would be unwise to do so, for such an approach, however deeply felt, "would have been construed as a meretricious merchandizing device."[49] He also felt so strongly against autographing the book that he told his publisher that he would not sign his name in copies. Writing to Ben Abramson, a

Chicago book dealer, Morley confided that "I feel so delicately and seriously about this book, and about Kitty Foyle as a human being (brave, lovely, and tormented by her own indecisions) that I could not, without a twinge of real embarrassment, write my name there except for close personal intimates."[50] Morley thought of his book as "a literary creation of deliberate restraint and form,"[51] and he had for its heroine a certain wry regard; in a letter to A. E. Newton, he spoke of his emotions toward Kitty: "Do you remember the very last words of Swift's *Journal to Stella* — 'Agreeable bitch, I said to myself.' "[52]

Attempting to give the book a special personality that was Kitty's alone, Morley altered his normal method of composition for *Kitty Foyle*. Previously he had written with a fountain pen, using it as a staff pen, dipping it into the bottle of ink to give himself sufficient time to choose his words; but Morley composed *Kitty Foyle* entirely on the typewriter. Beyond emphasizing Kitty's individuality, Morley hoped through this shift in his work methods "to keep it from being afflicted with literature and style." However, while the experiment may have simplified Morley's vocabulary somewhat, the style of *Kitty Foyle* remains unmistakably Morley's.

Another factor in the success of the novel is the memorable character of Kitty's father and the atmosphere of the Frankford district of Philadelphia which he personifies. "Pop" is a whiskey-drinking Irishman whose frequent curses — "Jesusgod" or, more politely, "Conshohocken" — punctuate his presence, as does his call for a bottle of Vat 69 whiskey: "the Pope's telephone number." His love for the game of cricket, as well as his great knowledge and experience as a coach, earn him the respect of the Main Line aristocrats, including Wyn. Frankford is evoked by such details as the backyard outhouse, smelling of chlorides and wisteria, and the battles with the black maid in the kitchen. In many ways *Kitty Foyle* develops the "sense of place" Morley thought so important.

Another consequence of this emphasis on place is the great amount of scene shifting which punctuates the novel. Kitty narrates the story of her life in an irregular sequence, beginning with her early years in Frankford, then jumping forward to her first year of high school with relatives in Manitou, Illinois. Several summers spent back in Frankford are then described together, followed by a return to Manitou for graduation. At this point Kitty recalls her return to Frankford for the summer and her abortive registration for college in Manitou which was cut short by her father's illness that necessitated another trip back to Frankford. While she is there, her affair with Wyn begins, and her father dies; she eventually leaves for New York to begin her career, with a side trip to Philadelphia for more of the affair. Two years in Chicago follow, with another excursion to Manitou, and a vacation in Bermuda where she meets Mark Eisen, the doctor she is thinking of marrying at the close of the book. While exciting, the constant changes of scene are, however, frequently confusing.

Despite its uniqueness among Morley's novels, *Kitty Foyle* does contain many of the elements common to all of his works. For example, references to Don Marquis and Shakespeare, taking their place even in the life of a working girl like Kitty, are ubiquitous, but they do document Morley's thesis that literature is vitally involved in people's lives. A strong dose of Morley's social philosophy is also present, including frequent mentions of the F. D. Roosevelt Brain Trusters and Socialism, about which Morley felt benevolently accepting. When Kitty, ensconced in New York to escape from Wyn, begins going with Mark Eisen, she says that "He knows damn well, what some of them don't yet, doctors and everything else that's important will get to be socialized sooner or later."[53] While Morley was hardly a political activist, he felt no special attachment to the existing economic order, and he occasionally made quite sanguine predictions about the eventual but quiet arrival of communal ownership. But *Kitty Foyle* is a tacit recognition of the power of class loyalties and social conditioning, for Kitty's passionate love for Wyn is eventually frustrated by the social gap between them.

Probably the most striking feature of the novel is the degree to which Christopher Morley, a male of nearly fifty years of age, was able to project himself into the character of Kitty. Although her thoughts sometimes wander into suspect intellectual depths, she remains very much a girl and, moreover, a distinctively modern one. Because her character is developed more thoroughly than that of any other Morley figure, her development enables the reader to empathize with her most unconventional decisions — such as her refusal to marry Wyn even though she is both pregnant and in love with him. Neither Kitty nor the book which bears her name ever lose their respective senses of humor. Compared to contemporary works with similar themes, such as Theodore Dreiser's *An American Tragedy*, *Kitty Foyle* projects a far greater sense of human reality; the characters are never caricatures, but complete people with small foibles and many-faceted personalities. And, while *Kitty Foyle* is in many ways far from Morley's "typical" novel, it is filled with the mature and benevolent philosophy that informs all of Morley's writings and is written with the same grace and erudition that Christopher Morley brought to all that he said and did.

VII   Thorofare

After the striking success of *Kitty Foyle*, Morley waited three years, until 1942, before bringing out his next novel, *Thorofare;* he seems to have lost his taste for the short, often humorous novels which he wrote at frequent intervals during his youth. While *Thorofare* demonstrates a considerable seriousness of purpose, it was not a commercial or literary success. It is overly long — 468 pages — and tries to cover too much ground by tracing in great detail the life of Geoffrey Barton from his English childhood to his American college graduation. Written during World War II, *Thorofare* was actually an attempt to bind Americans and Englishmen together by demonstrating their close spiritual ties.[54]

Reading this novel is a little like visiting well-loved, if somewhat dull, grandparents; *Thorofare* offers charm rather than stimulation, contemplation instead of violent action, and insight in place of passion. Morley demonstrates the subtle and varied relationships between Americans and Englishmen through a series of long, drawn-out incidents in the life of his main character, an English boy who comes to live in America. Although Morley was not born in England, his parents were, and he spent a portion of his childhood there during several summers. Thus, in writing about England, Morley drew largely on his own memories; he once called that country, "my grandmother."[55]

England is, in some senses, the heroine of *Thorofare*, since she is portrayed in loving detail, especially in the excessively long opening section of the book. It is through a group of English men and women, however, that she is portrayed in most of *Thorofare*. Morley inscribed his book, "For Uncles and Aunts," and these are, in fact, the characters most clearly realized in its pages. Geoffrey Barton, the ostensible main character, is less developed and memorable than his aunts Bee, Em, and Allie; his grandmother; and his Uncle Dan. These characters were patterned after Christopher Morley's own aunts Bertha, Edie, and Annie, and after his Grandmother Morley in the village of Woodbridge — called Wilford in the novel; Uncle Dan corresponds in many ways to his own father, Frank Morley, who left England for America in 1887.

Morley visited England, and Woodbridge in particular, on numerous occasions as a child, a college student, and a mature man. The spring he spent there in 1898, at the age of eight, brought back to him in later years recurring memories of Woodbridge, memories which he incorporated into *Thorofare:* "Walking round in the cold sunny air I thought, as always this time of year, of an old sunny brick wall espaliered with fruit trees in the long vanished family garden at Woodbridge. There, in early spring 1898, our governess Miss Downes used to take Felix and me to walk along the pathway."[56]

When, as a Rhodes scholar at Oxford, Morley revisited the town in 1911, he first became aware of the possibilities it held for a writer. On August 23 he noted in his journal: "There are several things I want to do in Woodbridge — to learn something about FitzGerald and Bernard Barton; to do some history reading; to see a bit of the country round Woodbridge; and to get to know picturesque Wood-bridge itself rather better." After reading Redstone's *Bygone Wood-bridge* in the local library and after asking his aunts to tell him about the Victorian poets who had sometimes come to visit the local celebrities, Morley resolved "to put down on paper my impressions of Woodbridge, as it is now, and the memories of the old house. . . ." One result of this effort was the early essay, "A Friend of FitzGerald," which was a character sketch of John Loder, the Wood-bridge bookseller who furnished the model for John Bredfield in *Thorofare.* Morley's return visits in 1925, 1926, and 1930 gave him ample opportunity to study the town, so that he was able to write about it convincingly in 1942, although he had not returned to England during the preceding twelve years.

Specific impetus for the novel came in July, 1940, from Jan Struthers, a British authoress who had recently arrived in America with her children on a ship that was evacuating British mothers and children from the dangers of the Blitz. Over ten thousand British children, Morley estimated, came to the United States in this way during 1940. Having only the month before purchased a home at Lloyd Harbor, Long Island, to house a British family, Morley was particularly receptive to Mrs. Struthers' suggestions that he write a novel emphasizing the closeness of the two nations, and they held more than one discussion on the subject. Although other writing duties kept Morley from actually beginning *Thorofare* until August, 1941, he then worked steadily on the book, finishing it in August, 1942. This period was not an easy one for Morley, or for anyone else in America, because with the war raging in Europe, it sometimes

seemed to Morley that the book might be in memory of England
rather than in homage. Nevertheless, while his son's life was en-
dangered in Africa, Morley continued to work on the book.

Thorofare is a long, discursive essay more than a novel; one section of ninety-two pages is devoted to a description of the eleven-day
voyage on which Geoffrey comes to America. Since Morley poured
into it his memories not only of England but also of his youth in
Baltimore, Geoffrey is in many ways an autobiographical
characterization. By the end of the novel the boy is largely
Americanized — his friends call him Jeff — but he returns to
England to study, realizing the hold his origins have on him. The
"Thorofare" of the title is not only the main street of Woodbridge,
but also the Atlantic Ocean, which Morley once called "the hero of
my novel — the ocean that is the thoroughfare between England
and ourselves, that bridges us together and that keeps us apart."[57]

Originally Morley had thought of the book as dedicated to the
memory of his parents; Frank Morley had died in 1937, and his wife
Lillian in 1939. Morley's mother, when dying, had asked one of her
sons, who was coming home from England, to bring her some
primroses. His father, walking with Christopher Morley in Woodbridge in 1911, had hummed the lines by Coleridge which were later
recited by Uncle Dan in *Thorofare:* "Is this the hill? Is this the kirk?
Is this mine own countree?" Morley's deep feeling for the book is illustrated by memorandum notations he made during its composition:

I see now that my true ambition is no less great, — to say something of the
old England I knew and its language and feeling — dedicated for FM &
LJM . . . Criterion: it would never have been told (Unless I told it).
                                                        — July 21, 1941

have to depend on my own memories: no one left to tell me about them —
while thinking of this comes news of FDR & Churchill meeting at sea — . . .
A[lfred] E[dward] N[ewton] saying on deathbed re England — if she goes
down she'll go nobly and leave a memory like ancient Greece —
                                                        — August —
                                                        — August 13, 1941

Attempting to clarify his style, Morley adopted a new method of
writing for *Thorofare:* he dictated to an amanuensis. Three days a
week he went to his New York office and dictated what he had
brooded upon during the preceding days; on those days when he was
not dictating, Morley also made notes and revised the typed copy
which his secretary had prepared. "I believe there is little doubt,"

Morley told an interviewer, "that this method has improved my writing. There is much less embroidery, much less loving fondling of words and phrasing, and so the story line is left clear and the story moves faster."[58] Despite Morley's statements, however, the book has little plot, and the narrative moves very slowly, especially toward the end. Whatever value the book has lies in the charming recreation of Victorian England in the long opening portion of the novel and in the accuracy with which Morley conveys the atmosphere of Baltimore in the early 1900's.

Thorofare is replete with the wordplay Morley enjoyed, including sage comments like "Woman, he thought, is a deponent verb: passive in form, but active in function." There is more of the identity between poetry and prose which appeared frequently in *Kitty Foyle:* Geoff's Uncle Dan, chopping wood, muses about "the twangling drone of the saw (cutting steadily into tough fiber, as language bites its way into meaning)." In a poem called "Sonnet in a Knothole," Morley describes his own wood-cutting:

> But no one guessed (we made no outward stopping)
> The sudden woodsman stroke that we incurred
> When down through fiber, grain, and knotted wit
> The oak of language shivered, cleanly split
> By the flashed ax-blade of the perfect word.[59]

Just as there is no divide between Morley's poetry and prose, he contends that neither is separate from the normal activities of real human beings.

Literature, in general, is wound up tightly in the plot of *Thorofare,* for Geoff's Uncle Dan, his guardian, is a professor of English literature at a small American college. The references to books and writing are constant and often witty. When Geoff's Southern girlfriend, Serena, reads him *The Tempest,* Morley comments that "always afterward . . . Jeff heard *The Tempest* in the soft accents of Chesapeake. And why not, he thought, Isn't it a Southren fable?" Jeff (now with the Americanized spelling) becomes an English major — of course — and is allowed to discover for himself all the books that Morley loved as an undergraduate, such as the works of Chaucer and the adventures of Sherlock Holmes. He puts out a juvenile journal, as Morley did, and dreams of becoming a writer.

Thorofare lacks a plot of compelling interest, as well as characterizations as accurately drawn as those of *Kitty Foyle*. It is, in many ways, almost the opposite of *Kitty Foyle:* tedious, excessively bookish, and with little inspiration beyond the understandable desire to bring America and England closer together. Christopher Morley's least attractive qualities are often exaggerated in *Thorofare*, and the novel consequently holds little appeal for most modern readers.

VIII   The Man Who Made Friends With Himself

Christopher Morley's last novel, *The Man Who Made Friends With Himself*, did not appear until 1949. The most carefully crafted of all Morley's novels, each sentence has been polished to an aphoristic shine, and every page is filled with paradoxes and humorous observations about life in postwar America. The main character, Richard Tolman, is an "authors' representative," or literary agent, a role Christopher Morley often played himself. As the epilogue reveals, "Tolman" is a shortened version of "Toulemonde," which not only suggests the French term for "everyone" but is also the title of a series of Morley poems.

The plot consists of a rather involved series of conversations and events during which Tolman sees, meets, and finally comes to terms with an elusive figure named Doppelganger, whom Tolman finally discovers to be his own double. This process is part of what Tolman refers to as "The Great Anxiety," and it is an attempt to create an allegory for the social and political problems of modern man. While this process of self-discovery is going on, Tolman is carrying on a serious love affair with a woman psychiatrist named Zoe Else and is having frequent conversations with his neighbor, Sharpy Cullen. The confrontation between Tolman and Doppelganger becomes increasingly tense; just as Tolman seems to have reconciled himself to his own personality and to the difficulties of living in the confused present, he is killed in a restaurant fire while trying to rescue his friend Sharpy — who has already escaped. The book is presented as a sort of journal kept by Tolman, and left in his safe for Zoe, "If anything ever happens to me. . . ."

Christopher Morley thought highly of his last novel; on various occasions he referred to it as "my brutal and heavenly book,"[60] "my beautiful and brutal novel,"[61] and "my best and sourest book."[62] Describing it to an interviewer, Morley said that he had a "feeling about it similar to the one Conrad had about *The Shadow Line* — often thought to be a neglected masterpiece — in which he made an attempt to be disastrously honest with himself and the reader."[63]

Perhaps the most interesting evidence of Morley's attitude toward his novel can be found in one of a series of advertisements that he wrote for *The Man Who Made Friends With Himself*, in which he described the book as "pure and shapely as an icicle, a dagger of despair." The significance of this description appears in the words of Richard Tolman in the novel: "Suppose, by some uproarious chance, that mss. . . . were what I always dreamed — pure and shapely as an icicle — a dagger of despair." Morley seems to imply that this was the book he had dreamed of writing.

"Eight years of thinking and four years of writing"[64] is how Morley described the gestation period of *The Man Who Made Friends*. . . . Diary notations indicate that he made some preliminary jottings as early as January, 1940, and that he gave additional thought to the book during the early 1940's but that serious work did not begin until March, 1945. The writing went slowly at first, with constant interruptions, so that by December, 1946, Morley had not finished the first section and had made a seventh fresh start. During the six months from February to August in 1947, he managed only about one hundred pages; but by September he had brought the total to twelve chapters of the thirty that were to constitute the whole. The final year of work, 1948, held still other difficulties, and Morley confided in March to a friend:

I have tried to learn, in these dreadful years, not to argue with anyone any more, or not too much more. I will pretend to agree about almost anything so as to get back sooner into my own blessed assurances. I am having such a gorgeous and horrible time with my wretched book that other affairs are only peripheral. I keep saying to myself, It must be beautiful; not too much mockery; yet mockery, if tender and detailed enough, is the sweetest of all beauty. . . . if the test of the artist is to begin from prostrate bottom, from anger & agony & despair, from apprentice fumbling and impossible stupor, then I might almost qualify. As you know, I don't even really much care any more if it gets published. Publishers think I'm being smart to duck so quick and so sideways, and I'm really just being humile. I don't even care about convincing anyone if I can only convince myself; the hardest of all.[65]

During the final year of work the manuscript grew longer than Morley wanted it, so ten weeks in the winter were spent in revision. He cut out twenty-five thousand words — about one-fifth of the whole — before deeming the book completed in December. It is easily understandable why he later said, "I have gone through more suffering, in writing this book, than I thought I could bear."[66]

One basic theme of the book is the importance of individualism, a concern of the author in many of his novels. While personal fulfillment was only a subsidiary concern in *Parnassus on Wheels*, Gissing in *Where the Blue Begins* left his home in search of the meaning of life; he eventually rejected answers based on public accomplishment. Phyllis and George Granville, in *Thunder on the Left*, tried desperately to be themselves; *Human Being*'s Richard Roe, stifled in his need for self-expression by an unhappy wife, found another woman who gave him back some of his self-esteem. Both Kitty Foyle and Uncle Dan of *Thorofare* were primarily self-motivated and self-regulated characters.

An interesting sidelight on the book is the source of Richard Tolman's elusive double, Doppelganger; for Morley had his own mysterious and elusive figure, who inspired the character in *The Man Who Made Friends*. . . . In the winter of 1939 Morley noted in his memorandum book, "the slender man I always see at Roslyn station and in subway, and makes no move to be known. His silence and self respecting or arrogant anonymity, in a world of chatterers, is one of my treasures." Morley again recorded seeing the anonymous commuter in the subway in June, 1941; this time he recorded that he was "startled and warned of MWMFWH." The most unusual encounter, however, did not occur until after the publication of the novel. Morley narrated the event in a letter to his friend Bill Gaffney, dated January 30, 1950:

I was severely shocked today: I had to go to Town, and on 43rd Street, just outside the back entrance of my bank (Corn Exchange on East 42 Street) I met the mysterious man I have seen for years on the LIRR trains, and who always rather gravelled me by never saluting me — I secretly always thought of him as That Man — he is a great polo player, and so graceful that every stride he takes is ballet; he spends as much time with horses as I do with books — and though I have watched & been snubbed by him for some 15 yrs I have never known who he is — and to my horror & startlement he waved to me. I was so accustomed to not being recognized by him, he was past before I could flap my arm. But that, I feel, is probably serious.

The love affair between Richard Tolman and Zoe Else is another of the main concerns of the novel. Zoe is an exceedingly modern — even liberated — heroine, of whom Tolman says, "loud cheers that her mind is as desirable as her body." Tolman claims that the two of them are able to "have more sport with some minor assiduity of grammar or philology than most people with a tureen of Spanish fly." The multidimensional character of the relationship is equally important to Zoe, who exclaims, "Why you old sweetheart, you make me think things I never thought of before. No one can do more for anyone than that."

Even more than in *Kitty Foyle*, which shocked so many readers with its premarital sex and abortion, Morley speaks frankly in *The Man Who Man Friends . . .* of the sexual side of human nature. One chapter involves a retrospective visit to a Philadelphia brothel; and Morley speaks frequently, if cautiously, of Richard and Zoe's physical relationship. In one chapter, a late afternoon conversation between the two is abandoned for what Morley calls "the deep, the deep embrace." Morley is equally concerned to describe how, after "the sweetness of body," there comes

. . . the sweetness of mind. Also the sweetness of a cigarette. I pulled the Venetian blinds so I could blow zeroes of smoke toward the radio programs. I even did the unforgivable, opened one of Zoe's dressing-table drawers, and found the box of kleenex. To open a woman's bureau will rouse her when nothing else will. She stirred. She was lovely moulding under a sheet, perfect as one of Lord Elgin's marbles. She whispered Love's consummate pitiful question: —

"Are you all right?"

The intimacy of their relationship is emphasized by an occasional ambiguity as to whom the book is speaking — a third-party reader, or Zoe. One example of this deliberate confusion occurs in the narration by Tolman of a strolling conversation: "Zoe is too smart to crack back. She just doubled ahead of me up the hill. You were wearing, I mean she was wearing . . . ." This touch should not be confusing to the reader since the introduction to the book explains that the manuscript has been written at least partially for Zoe by Tolman.

The setting of the novel, the village of "Wending Ways," is actually Roslyn, Long Island, where Morley lived for thirty-seven years. "Salamis Station," where Tolman catches his trains each morning, represents the Roslyn Station for the steam train of the Oyster Bay Branch of the Long Island Railroad; "Marathon" corresponds to Manhasset, the station for the electric train on the Westbury Branch. Tolman clearly delineates the "electric set" of commuters and the old-fashioned "steam folks" of the village, a distinction which Morley enjoyed making. "Wending Heights" stands for that part of the suburb known as Roslyn Heights (distinguished from Roslyn Estates) where Morley lived at "Green Escape," 41 The Birches.

In *The Man Who Made Friends With Himself*, Morley carefully portrays this small town on the "Long Gyeland Railroad," where commuters stride briskly to the station in the morning and, wilted, are picked up by their wives in station wagons in the late afternoon. Morley is eager to convey the natural beauty of the region where, at night in moonlight, "the birch trees stood up in slanted clusters, like white china muddling-rods in pools of absinthe," and where in the heat of day the tiger lilies seemed to burn in the sun.

As early as 1923 Morley had recorded in his journal his feeling for life in suburban Roslyn, in terms of youthful exuberance and enthusiasm: ". . . an occasional snake coiling on the warm highways, and gray-plumed squirrels; late last night a bat flittering about inside the house — little houses lying drowsily in the sunshine, among marigolds and the bright autumn flowers, and looking into green deepnesses of woodland . . . the best thing about Roslyn, I was thinking, is that it has no signs on the roads ROSLYN WELCOMES YOU and THANK YOU, COME AGAIN as do most of the villages hereabouts — Roslyn seems sufficient to itself. . . ." This awareness of suburban life became, twenty-five years later, the deep feeling that informed *The Man Who Made Friends* . . . with the same sort of local color that permeates Dylan Thomas' *Under Milk Wood*. With an almost Joycean inclusiveness, Morley tried in his last novel to present the particulars of Roslyn life as symbolic of life everywhere. During that twenty-five-year span both Roslyn and Morley had matured, and Morley's vision of Roslyn was far less sentimental in 1949.

This sharp sense of place, as well as the interest Morley had in the lives of the residents of his village, are reflected by Richard Tolman's acute consciousness of even those characters who are totally uninvolved in the literature which is the center of his own life. Thinking of his fellow commuters, Tolman is amazed "by casual things they say, casual bundles they carry, their patient fidelity and good humor, the daily discipline of their collars and stockings." These characters include E. E. Allibone, who wears heavy South American silk pajamas with his initials on the pocket; Frank Xerxes Mullaly, the road commissioner who becomes considerate of the residents only when up for re-election; Tolman's booming neighbor, Sharpy Cullen; and Sharpy's wife Betty, who faces middle age with the comment, "I used to be the youngest person there ever was."

There is much wordplay and punful humor in *The Man Who Made Friends With Himself:* Tolman walks a "trodbare rug" as he dictates; he speaks of the "Irrev. Laurence Sterne"; Sharpy Cullen's grandchildren "rump around" in the sandpile; and in the garden, fireflies were "morseing about." Unusual similes vivify Morley's descriptions: "I saw a stocky bee, very like a Minnesota halfback, plunging head-long into the roses as though looking for holes in the Wisconsin line." Frequent aphorisms, such as "Study your own anguish before you presume to relieve others'. If you have no anguish of your own, hurry to find one," punctuate the conversations of Morley's characters. Old words are used in new ways; describing his passage through a crowd, Tolman claims that, "I minnow through the shoal"; the catbirds "beak out" bugs and wood-lice from a mouldering log.

The Man Who Made Friends With Himself is the most intensely literary of all Morley's novels, as well as one of the most demanding to read. It utilizes the entire range of Morley's immense vocabulary and erudition, as well as incorporating many autobiographical episodes. Constant allusions to the language and ideas of great writers support Morley's contention that "Language, the varied vulgate of common men, is our greatest glory."[67] He paraphrases Kipling to describe the newspapers as "Just Not So Stories"; when caught in a Manhattan crowd, Tolman thinks of the river in Joyce's *Finnegan's Wake:* "Weh, oh Weh! Silly to be flowing but I no canna stay." A chapter on commuting trains evokes a quotation from *King Lear* by Tolman: "A little to disquantity your train." Tolman's friend Sharpy Cullen is dismayed to hear from Tolman that he has quoted Boswell entirely by accident; Morley insists that "That's what is cruel about literature, it says things before they happen."[68] More tightly than in any other Morley work, life and literature are glued together in *The Man Who Made Friends With Himself.* There is recognition that literature, and writers, can be as absurd and foolish as life itself: Tolman remarks that, "I live a long way This Side Idolatry; even Chaucer and Conrad could be corny."[69]

In many ways the most mature of Morley's works, *The Man Who Made Friends With Himself* is also the most skeptical, at least in its attitudes toward human society. Tolman, a man of about Morley's age in the late 1940's, admits that "I think it quite possible that humanity intends to go on, but I will have nothing responsible to do with prolonging such confusion." Having lived and written through two world wars, Morley seems to have developed a protective disbelief in the world of politics and international affairs: "I was reading poetry that night — I do, about once a week, to take me back to reality after the folklore of the evening papers."[70] However, as the title indicates, Tolman eventually reconciles himself with his own personality and society; this reconciliation seems to be Morley's prescription for what he called "The Peace of Nerves."

Unless modern man could come to terms with himself and transcend his rhetoric and his politics, Morley had little faith in society's ability to either improve or continue. The ambiguous but tragic ending, in which Tolman and his black housekeeper's son both die in a restaurant fire, seems to be intended as a warning against the perilous tensions that threaten humanity. Tolman saw signs of impending disaster in unusual places: "My life was difficult because I loved words. I perceived their terrible power; I tried not to mollify their meanings. Their overproduction and misuse are the stigmata of our perishing culture."[71] Language was paramount to Morley; he regarded salvation for society as dependent, therefore, upon its ability to speak clearly and honestly to itself.

Like his other late novels, *The Man Who Made Friends With Himself* is replete both with poetry, attributed to Richard Tolman, and with literally poetic lines — passages which become, almost verbatim, poems. Early in the novel, Tolman makes a kind of daily prayer of some lines of Robert Herrick; Morley's poem, "The Nightpiece to Herrick," begins,

> O Herrick, parson of my heart
> I'll go to church with thee,
> And bear a humble willing part
> In thy sweet liturgy.[72]

A conversation with Sharpy Cullen produces the lines, "The nymph Calypso is a bit of a dipso, she can't keep up her drawers they slip so." This doggerel becomes the first verse of "Forever Ambrosia," a Morley poem about the *Odyssey*. Richard Tolman notes that "even dogs can sublimate; they don't bark at the milkman." Similarly, one of the "Toulemonde" poems is subtitled, "Dogs Don't Bark at the Milkman." The phrase seems to have symbolized to Morley the natural basis for civilization offered by enlightened self-interest. The line between poetry and prose is, once again, as thin as that between literature and life. Tolman's nieces, Gin and Ginger, are talking about books with their uncle:

> "How I loath that word *literature*," they cried. "Isn't it only what people would have said to each other if they'd had a chance?"
> "And then they went ahead and said it anyhow."[73]

Christopher Morley seems to have guessed that *The Man Who Made Friends With Himself* would be his last novel. He reprints, with only slight alterations, a memorandum which he wrote late in 1947 in the body of the novel as a Tolman late-night *pensée:* "I believe I have led, and now gently retreat from, the happiest life among all men I have known. I grabbed and guzzled it sometimes, without delicacy or dignity. In those burning wastelands of the night, that purer men never endured, I've had my willyways. But take it by and large, all and sundry, we have lived our own, our very own, absurd and vulgar joy. We have cried, in moments not exceeded by Shakespeare, nor Shelley, nor Tally, plain expletives of mirth."[74]

The Man Who Made Friends With Himself embodies much of what was weakest and strongest in Morley's novels: they are often the same thing. This novel is so intensely personal that it can be fully understood only by someone familiar with Morley's life and other works. It is so extravagantly allusive and rich with quotation that it has limited appeal to anyone not at least partially a bibliophile like Morley. At the same time, its thematic content is significant and well developed, and its finely polished style provides a banquet for lovers of the English language. *The Man Who Made Friends With Himself* is clearly one of Christopher Morley's most important works, but it lacks the wide public appeal that made *Kitty Foyle* a best seller.

Christopher Morley's novels show a kind of progression from the earliest to the last, for they become more and more sophisticated in what Morley brought to them and in what he demanded of his readers. At the same time, the issues and themes of Morley's late novels were often present in his first: it is only the development and the tone that have changed. For example, virtually all of his novels follow the "Morley Manifesto," which he announced in *Parnassus on Wheels*, to bring great literature to the common man. Most stress the individuality of the main characters, emphasizing the need for each human being to determine for himself what is most important in his life. All demonstrate how careful observation of even the smallest details and events in a human life can be of paramount importance.

While these themes are constant in Morley's novels, the tone becomes both more urban and more urbane in the later ones. Roger Mifflin, Morley's first protagonist, is involved with literature, to be sure, but his very independent individualism is largely a function of his rough-hewed, frontier quality. Richard Tolman of *The Man Who Made Friends With Himself*, on the other hand, is a man of understated sophistication, commuting from his suburban home to his job in New York City, carrying on a love affair with an attractive professional woman, and keeping a journal full of insights into modern society.

Similarly, Morley's early novels were, on the whole, brief in length and displayed simple plot and character developments. Not until *Human Being* did Morley produce a book endowed with the degree of character development and the breadth of plot that we expect today from a mature novelist. Only in *Kitty Foyle* — and then partly by restraining his bibliophiliac tendencies — did Morley produce a novel that genuinely matched the temper of the nation, without abandoning the "concerns," to use a favorite Morley term, which motivated his other works.

What makes Morley's novels so interesting and unusual as a group is their unwavering conviction, variously expressed, that literature is not only relevant but essential to human life. The lives of virtually all Morley protagonists are tied to books or writing in some way — how could they be alive otherwise, Morley seems to ask? Thus Christopher Morley's novels are not essentially "escape" literature, although they sometimes serve that purpose as well: most importantly, they are both examples of and arguments for the real presence of literature in the lives of average human beings. Morley's style was especially congenial to this venture, for it enabled him to mix great erudition with playful humor in a unique blend. While he used his novels as vehicles for his convictions about the importance and vitality of words and books, he simultaneously created literature of importance which reached a considerable portion of the reading public of his day.

CHAPTER 4

Poetry

If he could have his druthers
  Every poet knows
He would avoid the bothers
  Of writing careful prose.

For in his verse he gathers
  Such music, such finesse,
Unwrung remain his withers
  If it never goes to press.

O secret poets, brothers!
  Ourselves rereading still —
We know how few, few others
  Ever will.[1]

L ATE in his career Christopher Morley was able to adopt
  this gently mocking tone toward his own poetry — aware,
however, that, while he enjoyed writing poems more than anything
else, his poetry was the least "appreciated" aspect of his work. Both
Morley's first book, *The Eighth Sin*, and his last, *Gentlemen's
Relish*, were collections of poems; he published, in total, eighteen
volumes of poetry; and he included selections of his poems in four
other works — the line between Morley's prose and poetry was never
very firm. He confessed that "I have never been completely happy
except when writing verse. I've the horridest feeling that after it's
too late for me, someone will say, 'He wrote poetry.' "[2] When he was
asked by Whit Burnett to submit some of his writing for an
anthology entitled *This Is My Best*, Morley gave him four poems,
saying "I hope it will not startle you if I say I think I should prefer to
enter your caravan as a poet rather than in other possible disguises
. . . poetry was and remains my first love."[3]

One of those poems included in Morley's contribution to Burnett's anthology was the opening poem of the 1923 collection *Parson's Pleasure*. Entitled "Of a Child That Had Fever," it is one of his finest verses:

> I bid you, mock not Eros
>   Lest Eros mock with you.
> His is a hot distemper
>   That hath no feverfew.
>
> Love, like a child in sickness,
>   Brilliant, languid, still,
> In fiery weakness lying,
>   Accepts, and hath no will.
>
> See, in that warm dispassion
>   Less grievance than surprise,
> And pitiable brightness
>   In his poor wondering eyes.
>
> Oh delicate heat and madness,
>   Oh lust unnerved and faint:
> Sparkling in veins and fibers,
>   Division and attaint!
>
> I bid you, mock not Eros;
>   He knows not doubt or shame,
> And, unware of proverbs,
>   The burnt child craves the flame.[4]

I *General Characteristics*

Morley's poetry was generally traditional in construction, including a large number of sonnets; but he created a quite successful form of his own which he called "Translations from the Chinese." His poetic work, therefore, is most practically treated in two parts: the traditional body of poems, and the more original genre. All of Morley's poetry, and especially his conventional work, reflects his predominant concern with literature; consequently, many of his poems deal with the problems of writing poetry, and many others treat the lives and works of other poets. He was aware that he was a distinctly "minor" poet, but he found advantage in that category: "I mean that the best way to tune in on great poets is to be a small poet yourself."[5] Many critics admired Morley's poetic works: Elinor

Wylie called him "a latterday Herrick"; William Rose Benét, who compared some Morley poems to Ralph Waldo Emerson's works, called his "Toulemonde" series "the most quietly succulent asparagus of the mind."[6]

One of the most important characteristics of Morley's poetic voice is his use of specific detail. A carefully observant man, he took a poet's proprietary interest in the particulars of the natural world, constantly noticing small things; he was always willing to follow a side street, to admire the shape of an unusual nose, or to listen to the varied dialects filling Manhattan Island. Because of this natural curiosity, Morley was able to impart to his readers such a wealth of captured images that he encouraged others to see the world freshly themselves.

This detail was discovered in both city and country. Working in his garden, the poet narrates how "heart and I" idled and observed their surroundings:

> We watched the puddle lose its glaze of frost,
> Measured the April in a pale March sky
> And saw the birch-tree all newly mossed.
> Filling our fingernails with Spring, we raked
> And burned and swept, and breathed, and chopped some wood;
> And even in that easiness, heart ached
> To keep this noon forever, if we could.[7]

When "freshcut grass smelled sweet as cinnamon," the poet heard in his swamp the frogs, "whistlingales of boyhood joy." Near by sat beloved pets, a cat with "pointed ear and petal toe," and an old spaniel who "rubs white chaps and floating ears/ In summersweet suburban loam." As fall arrives, Morley tells how, "chattering voltage like a broken wire/ The wild cicada cried, Six weeks to frost." A detail of winter is captured as Morley notes that one of the virtues of snow is that it "makes brick steps wonderfully pink when you sweep them."

The details of city life are given equal attention. Fascinated by the electric news bulletin in Times Square, Morley forgets to read the message due to his absorption with the period "swimming along at the tail of the sentence/ Like a baby goldfish/ Trying to catch up." He tells how, one October day, tiny milkweed fluffs were blown into town from Hackensack meadows so that "all day long/ On busy street corners/ Men reached to grasp the drifting gauzes/ With twinges they couldn't explain." And he gently discloses "a crosstown street/ In sunset parallel/ Where lovers lay in peace so sweet/ They never heard the El." One of the characteristics, then, of many of Morley's best poems is this careful use of specific detail; in this respect, one of his primary aims as a writer was to convey the particular joy he felt at many minor occurrences; in one poem, he concluded, "I wanted to tell *you* how beautiful it was." By concentrating on the specific, rather than on the general and the abstract, Morley hoped to transmit his particular vision of the world. A final example of this characteristic is the last section of "The Watchman's Sonnet." Remaining on the job in a darkened library, the watchman is startled by a strange sight in the dawn after a night filled with rain and then fog:

> Sideways he saw a flash, a speeding thing —
> Lightning? He startled for the thunder-crack,
> Then knew what flickered past the window pane:
> Daylight, replenished on a bird's wet wing.[8]

A second characteristic of Morley's poetry is his inventive use of analogy — an inventiveness that he developed. Conscious of the fact that we have only one chance to see things, Morley related in "A Lesson" how he once wanted to return and study some unusual ice formations he had seen, but he held himself back from doing so since he was attempting to teach himself to observe and was aware that "we can't always go back for another look." Samples of the analogies Morley included in his poems are the "little flickering period" of the Times Square sign, about which he remarked, "I have a horrid thought, that's Me"; and his observation that coal and ice are always sold by the same merchant indicating "the irremediable duplicity of the world" by a sort of Hegelian antithesis. Once when he was enjoying the beauty of the night, and imagining that the thrill of the crickets constituted a kind of "haiku" poem in itself, an electric light bulb went out; his imaginative analogy drawn from the experience was that "the bulb went out on purpose to teach me/ Not to take the translation for the original."

Simile and metaphor are among the techniques used by a poet like Morley, one susceptible to the force of analogy. Thus, to Morley, the Baltimore oriole warbling his lyric, "Why do you work, why?/ Why? Why work?" seemed to be "Malvolio from Maryland." Staying in the city for the winter, the poet is awakened at night by cars rushing down his street; his "country ears, quicker than reason" deceive him; and he thinks, "What a wind has risen/ Among my tall strong trees." The processes of writing, as well, suggest to him metaphorical comparisons:

The Epigram

To write an epic or a novel
  Seems straightforward work to me —
By conscientious indentation
  The beaver bevels down the tree;

But, with the imprecisive arrow
  The intended acorn fairly struck—
Such is epigram, requiring
  Wit, occasion, and good luck!

Other unique comparisons abound in Morley's poems: the fuss that men make about their planet reminds him "of the staff of a humorous weekly/ Sitting in grave conference on a two-line joke"; life sometimes seems to him a game of whist between Man and Nature in which Nature holds the trump card, "the mating instinct." In one poem which makes extensive use of analogy, "Ammonoosuc," a New England river becomes, for the poet, "both parable and fact"; finding it during a crucial period of his life, when he needed reassurance, Morley swam in the river and was both pysically and spiritually refreshed. The experience suggested to him that "every heart in every land/ Has its own Ammonoosuc." One of the aims of the poem is to establish a meaningful analogy between the natural setting and the mood of the poet, a distinctly Romantic concept.

Aware of his tendency to find "tongues in trees, books in brooks," and "sermons in stones," Morley wryly commented upon his frequent analogizing in "Pragmatism," one of his "Translations from the Chinese":

When Chancellor Mu Kow and I were ennuyés
We used to go to the windy hill
And fly paper kites.
"Have you considered, Tremendous One"
(I asked him),
"The paradox of the kite?
To make it soar steadily

> You must weight it down with a tail;
> And to keep the spirit lofty, it is well . . ."
> —"Do not, I beg you"
> (Replied the Great Magistrate)
> "Unsettle me with analogies.
> You have only to meditate and watch the goldfish,
> I must govern a province."[9]

Unsettling as the analogies may occasionally be, Morley's were useful in helping his readers see otherwise hidden sides to ordinary objects and in stimulating them to make similar discoveries on their own.

II Morley's Early Poems

Both while at Haverford College and at Oxford, Christopher Morley wrote a good deal of poetry. In 1912, while he was at Oxford, he began his published career in the midst of what has since been recognized as the modern renaissance of English poetry:

So far as I was concerned the Renaissance began one spring morning when (as usual) I went down three flights of stone stairs, in dressing gown and pajamas, to see if there was any mail on the slab at the bottom. There was a letter from *T. P.'s Magazine*. Here it is (you don't think I would have lost that letter) —

8th May, 1912

The Editor of *T. P.'s Magazine* would be pleased to use Mr. Morley's poem entitled "Rondeau" if he would accept 7/6d for same.

That was the first time I was ever paid money for writing anything.[10]

By that autumn Morley had accumulated enough poems for the proverbially slim first volume. Sixty pages long and bound in bluish-gray paper, *The Eighth Sin* was printed in an edition of 250 copies. Its contents were uniformly juvenile, many directed to "the Only Begetter," a young American girl named Helen Fairchild whom Morley had met the previous year in London and later married. Of the booklet Morley later reminisced, "The perpetrator, if he thinks of it at all, thinks of it fondly as a boy's straggling nosegay, somewhat wilted in a hot eager hand, clumsily tied together with honest love."[11]

When Morley returned to America in 1913 and married Miss Fairchild the following year, his verse took an emphatically domestic turn. The titles of these early collections include *Songs for a Little*

House, The Rocking Horse, Hide and Seek, and *Chimneysmoke.*
The word that Morley coined to describe these early efforts, but that
some critics picked up as a term of abuse, was "dishpantheism."[12]
While a large number of these poems seem impossibly sentimental
and naive today, Morley defended them, saying "To the devil with
those who pretend to ridicule sentiment. There is room for
enlightened sentiment, aerated by humor, stiffened with irony and
self mockery, but not devoid of compassion."[13] Perhaps the best
known of all Morley's domestic poems is the widely reprinted
"Animal Crackers," which begins

> Animal Crackers, and cocoa to drink,
> That is the finest of suppers, I think;
> When I'm grown up and can have what I please
> I think I shall always insist upon these.[14]

In addition to the homely sentiment, these early collections often
demonstrated the literary bent that Morley's poems increasingly
took in later works. "At the Mermaid Cafeteria," for example, was
one of Morley's best received early works:

> Truth is enough for prose:
> Calmly it goes
> To tell just what it knows.
>
> For verse, skill will suffice—
> Delicate, nice
> Casting of verbal dice.
>
> Poetry, men attain
> By subtler pain
> More flagrant in the brain —
>
> An honesty unfeigned,
> A heart unchained
> A madness well restrained.[15]

Another early poem, "The Poet," which criticized the writer who
was "Artist merely in his rhyme,/ Not in his life,"[16] pursued the
favorite Morley theme that literature apart from real life was hardly
worthy of being considered art. Morley combined his literary and
domestic veins in a humorous poem entitled "To a Very Young
Gentleman," which parodies Rudyard Kipling's "If":

If you can think up seven thousand methods
Of giving cooks and parents heart disease;
Can rifle pantry-shelves, and then give death odds
By water, fire, and falling out of trees;

If you can fill your every boyish minute
With sixty seconds' worth of mischief done,
Yours is the house and everything that's in it,
And, which is more, you'll be your father's son![17]

III *Literary Poetry*

Christopher Morley, who wrote surprisingly many poems about other poets, frequently focused on certain personal favorites. Keats, for example, was treated in an early work which contrasted his own tortured life with those of the young men who sit "Perfectly happy . . . talking about Keats."[18] When a letter of Keats's to Fanny Brawne was auctioned in 1920, Morley wrote "In An Auction Room" to commemorate the occasion. A later work, "Hampstead Coach," was considered by poet William Rose Benét, to be "one of the best poems about Keats."[19] Walter De La Mare chose Morley's sonnet, "Charles and Mary," as one of the twenty-four he included in his 1950 *Saturday Book;* the poem is based on several lines from a letter describing Charles Lamb's relationship with his sister:

I hear their voices still: the stammering one
Struggling with some absurdity of jest;
Her quiet words that puzzle and protest
Against the latent outrage of his fun.
So wise, so simple — has she never guessed
That through his laughter, love and terror run?
For when her trouble came, and darkness pressed,
He smiled, and fought her madness with a pun.

Through all those years it was his task to keep
Her gentle heart serenely mystified.
If Fate's an artist, this should be his pride —
When, in that Christmas season, he lay dead,
She innocently looked. "I always said
That Charles is really handsome when asleep."[20]

Still another early work, "O. Henry — Apothecary," treats a real episode in that American writer's life. "Alexander Pope, 1688 - 1744" is a sonnet which emphasizes Pope's polemical powers:

> POPE, who loved his rhymes in duplicates,
> Chose couplets also for his mortal dates:
> Born '88, precisian to the core,
> Died, of exactitude, in '44.
>
> Duplex himself, both wasp and honey-bee:
> The wasp whose sting was immortality;
> The bee whose nectar, sugared in the cyst,
> Could turn to fury in a paper nest.
>
> When Pope lit on the bare hide of a dunce
> He did not need to do so more than once.
> It was no use to rub the place with soap.
> The only lucky fools were born since Pope.
>
> Most perfect mind in English, he had fun:
> Assassin and embalmer, both in one.[21]

"Atomic Fission, April 1387," and "Ballade of an Old Friend" are poems which memorialize Chaucer, one of Morley's true gods: "Hail Chaucer, dearest of them all."[22] A very late poem, "Ballade of the Welkin," is built around one line from Chaucer's *Troilus and Criseyde*, the same work that inspired Morley's *The Trojan Horse*: "The welkin shope him for to reyne."[23] "Dorothy" is a tribute to the patience and intelligence of Wordsworth's sister which concludes "Only the very wise would guess whose poems they really were."[24] In "To Luath" Morley even devotes a poem to Robert Burns's dog, because of whom Burns met Jean Armour.

"Episodes in the Arts" is a late series of poems from *Spirit Level* which takes a somewhat different approach to writers and other artists. Quoting short descriptions of Lord Byron, John Ruskin, John Millais, Praxiteles, and Toulouse-Lautrec, Morley proceeded to write short poems taking off on those characters. Leigh Hunt's autobiography that mentioned Byron's living habits inspired Morley to write:

> Except when chasing someone's daughter
> Byron lived on gin and water;
> Fearful of the nickname Fatso
> Ate small meals in his palazzo.[25]

"Three Approximations" varies that pattern of rhymed couplets slightly, building short poems, actually extremely free-verse renderings, on Latin verses from Horace, Martial, and Catullus.[26]

Many other poems were dedicated to, or referred to, the works of other poets and writers. "Nursery Rhymes for the Tender-Hearted," for example, is dedicated to Don Marquis; it deals humorously with the adventures of a roach patterned after Marquis's famous "archy."[27] A lengthy series of couplets about famous Elizabethan writers is contained in Morley's poem, "To His Mistress, Deploring That He Is Not An Elizabethan Galaxy." In this poem, typical verses include, "I creak my rhymes up like a derrick,/ I ne'er will be a Robin Herrick," and "My wits are dull as an old Barlow — / I wish that I were Christopher Marlowe."[28] (This last wish was, in fact, relatively easy to fulfill, since "Morley" is an Elizabethan variant of "Marlowe.") An obituary for Austin Dobson, "a writer of light verse," became a poem which also describes much of Morley's work:

> Tenderest trifles! how he caught
> (So charmingly, so many times)
> The swift, reluctant birds of thought
> In the bright cages of his rhymes.[29]

A poem remembering Morley's happy days in England as a Rhodes scholar was not only dedicated but addressed to Rupert Brooke, concluding "To think that while these joys I knew/ In Cambridge, I did not know you."[30] The 300th Anniversary of Herrick's "Hesperides" inspired a 1948 Morley poem; so did a portrait of Dr. Samuel Johnson.[31]

"Elected Silence: Three Sonnets" was written in memory of Morley's friend William Rose Benét, who died in 1950; a combination of sadness, faith, and humor, it memorializes a man who had collaborated on one of Morley's last volumes of poetry, a collection of the two men's works called *Poetry Package*, which appeared in 1950 and which has an intriguing history.

When Morley first came to New York in 1913, he had been struck by an advertisement in a magazine he had bought to read on the train; the advertisement had promoted the sale of a book of poems, *Merchants of Cathay*, by William Rose Benét. Morley wondered to himself, "would it ever be possible for me also to get some poems printed, and maybe even to meet, just once and a while, men of printed poems and musical names. . . ."[32] He met Benét in the early 1920's, and they became friends. Then, in 1949, another advertisement attracted Morley's attention. Among books offered by a large New York department store in a "Sale of the Unsalable" were a collection of poems by Benét and one by himself; they were offered together as a "Poetry Package" for a dollar. This marketing gimmick inspired Morley to suggest that the two poets select their favorites from among each other's recent poems and have them published in a paperback volume as their own bargain offer.

When *Poetry Package* reached the public, the co-authors were identified on the cover and on the title page by only their initials; inside, the poems were variously attributed to "Dove Dulcet" and "Pigeon Cove," pseudonyms that the authors had used previously. An introductory essay, signed "Cuckoo" to continue the bird motif, was written by critic Chauncey Brewster Tinker. The cover carried caricatures of the two poets as birds: Benét, as a pigeon operating a typewriter with his toe; Morley, as a bearded and bespectacled dove writing with a quill pen. After the book was published, Morley told a reporter that it had been printed in sesquicentennial salute to the memory of Wordsworth and Coleridge and their *Lyrical Ballads* of 1798. "We're a year late," Morley admitted in 1949, "but we thought of it last year."[33] In reality, they were more than a year late since *Poetry Package* was issued on January 1, 1950, by Morley's friend and associate, Louis Greenfield.

Morley's relationship with Benét was a close one; in the last of three sonnets in "Elected Silence," some of the flavor of that friendship can, perhaps, be felt:

> So . . . so . . . each poet has his secret faith
> That somewhere, somewhen, someone might arise,
> Might read him with unfashionable eyes,
> Critic uncrazed by momentary scathe,
> So skilled in loves or laughters and/or lust
> Dissects the formal flaky pastrycrust
> To our god-orchard deepdish fruit below. . . .
> And now no postage-stamp will let you know.
> We saw men in their universal blitz
> Tear our bicycle-boyhood world to bits,
> Yet also saw tree, ocean surf, and hill
> In the morn's morning measured fresh and new.
> My faith, such as it is (not much), dear Bill
> Is partly faith in you.[34]

An equally large number of Christopher Morley's poems were addressed not so much to individual poets and writers as to the profession of writing itself. Books, Morley's most enduring love, are the subject of this fairly late poem:

In A Second-Hand Bookshop

> What waits me on these shelves? I cannot guess,
>   But feel the sure foreboding; there will cry
> A voice of human laughter or distress,
>   A word that no one needs as much as I.
>
> For always where old books are sold and bought
>   There comes that twinge of dreadful subtlety —
> These words are actual, and they were thought
>   By someone who was once alive, like me.[35]

"Lines For An Eccentric's Book Plate" was an early effort of Morley's to express the related theme that books were meant to be lived and to be treated as integral parts of the lives of real people.[36] "The Watchman's Sonnet," written under a pseudonym for the fiftieth anniversary of the Columbia University Press, compares books with the daylight that relieves the dark, proclaiming that "Since men learned print, no night is wholly black."[37] The humorous "Shakespeare in Junior High" claims that literature speaks most clearly to the reader who sees it as relevant to his own life:

> I'm reading Shakespeare, Fourteen Years confessed:
> He's tops! I don't suppose in Junior High
> We get it all: but gee, I like him best
> When he writes about Me. He makes me cry!
> Could I say that, in my English test?
>
> Say it; and you, musicians of the spheres
> Know that your glory never was so great
> As when our humble parallel appears,
> And in the Universal agony
> You recognize, condone, and sublimate
> The all-devouring all-transmuting Me.
>
> Bespeak us when we were savage, young, and pure:
> When we lived, not studied, literature:
> Sonnets not fourteen lines, but fourteen years.[38]

A similar message, although one more sentimentally expressed, is worked into "To A Child," where Morley asserts that

> The greatest poem ever known
> Is one all poets have outgrown:
> The poetry, innate, untold,
> Of being only four years old.[39]

The problems of writing poetry, or simply of writing at all, appear constantly in Christopher Morley's verses. While *Religio Journalistici* is Morley's prose farewell to journalism, "A Grub Street Recessional" serves the same purpose in Kiplingesque rhyme:

> O noble gracious English tongue
> Whose fibres we so sadly twist,
> For caitiff measures he has sung
> Have pardon on the journalist.
>
> For mumbled metre, leaden pun,
> For slipshod rhyme, and lazy word,
> Have pity on this graceless one —
> Thy mercy on Thy servant, Lord!
>
> The metaphors and tropes depart,
> Our little clippings fade and bleach:
> There is no virtue and no art
> Save in straightforward Saxon speech.
>
> Yet not in ignorance or spite,
> Nor with Thy noble past forgot
> We sinned: indeed we had to write
> To keep a fire beneath the pot.
>
> Then grant that in the coming time,
> With inky hand and polished sleeve,
> In lucid prose or honest rhyme
> Some worthy task we may achieve —
>
> Some pinnacled and marbled phrase,
> Some lyric, breaking like the sea,
> That we may learn, not hoping praise,
> The gift of Thy simplicity.[40]

"Interruptions," subtitled (an Essay in Verse), describes the traumas afflicting various writers attempting to compose: Shakespeare, completing *The Tempest*, is summoned by his wife to aid in disposing of a mouse; Alfred Lord Tennyson is distracted from his idylls to assist in a birth; Thomas Jefferson's efforts to write the Declaration of

Independence are frustrated by the family dogs; finally, Morley concludes,

> There is one horror makes all writers kin,
> Drives them to stomach ulcers or to gin:
> Interruption, their poor alibi
> For not writing things that never die.
> But even more ridiculous and sad,
> Those who lived so sheltered that they never had
> Domestic uproar, or a telephone call,
> Were never heard of at all.[41]

Typically, life is essential to art for Morley: it may be distracting, but it cannot be shut out without vitiating art. In "While Revising Some Verses," Morley asks, "Here in a sky so pure, weather so sweet/ How can a verse endure/ Fit to compete?"; but he finishes by announcing that "Silence is exquisite—/ And yet . . . and yet . . ."[42]

More quotidian considerations of writing are treated in Christopher Morley's "Sonnet on Copyright," where he determines that his sonnet will be ". . . or else the law is nix,/ Copyright, until 2-0-0-6."[43] "And A Crooked Tree," otherwise a lovely lament by an aging poet, tells the reader ironically that "I had good advice for men's despair:/ You can find it exactly where/ I said it. Most of it's o.p."[44] (That is, out of print, as Morley informs the reader in a footnote.) "Go, Little Verse" is a playful lyric about a poem that came out quite contrary to the author's original intent; Morley ends it laconically: "Sweet are the uses of a pseudonym."[45] In another poem, "Epitaph On The Proofreader of the Encyclopedia Britannica," Morley indicates that he "perished, obstinately brave:/ They laid the Index on his grave."[46] The least romantic aspect of literature, printing, is celebrated in "A Printer's Madrigal."[47]

IV   Toulemonde

As we have indicated, special notice should be given the series of poems that Morley entitled "Toulemonde." The first volume bearing that name was a collection of verse and song interspersed; it was not particularly successful. Later, however, in *The Middle Kingdom*, Morley added three new Toulemonde poems which reflect his feelings about himself and about the world he found in his later years; he does so much like the character Richard Tolman in *The Man Who Made Friends With Himself*. The first poem of this later series, "Toulemonde Desipient," is a cheerful, relaxed sequence of verses; the last stanza reads:

> The feeling of a day when nothing has to be done:
> No appointments, absolutely none,
> Just to loiter along the shelves;
> And then, when everyone's in bed,
> The silence overhead.
>
> *His blue morocco slippers donned,*
> *What evenings then had Toulemonde.*

"Toulemonde: The Golden Germ" celebrates a recovery from infection by *staphylococcus aureus*, literally a "golden germ." The infected Toulemonde thinks to himself while ill,

> Then you're not so keen about autonomy
> And prefer a planned economy.
> Free competition doesn't seem so right
> Between *staphylococcus* and phagocyte.

The longest poem of the series and the last one, "Toulemonde: Intermezzo," pays an ironic tribute to the pleasures of middle age:

> Here is a song (O dry those tears)
> In honor of man's Middle Years —
> Unmusical, more like a shout;
> But what's the yodeling about?
> It's *fun* to grow old . . . if the guts hold out.
>
> Steward? — Steward! Another snort
> While I make my interim report.
> My gums recede, my belly pouts,
> I feel mysterious pangs and gouts
> And frequent philosophic doubts
>
> . . . .
>
> But sagged in front or tweaked behind
> All the more ecstasy I find
> In the employment of the mind.
>
> Still, thank God, are gorgeous days
> When thought kindles to a blaze

On some unearned chrysostom phrase,
Or, with equal pleasure, sags
Upon unmentionable gags

. . . .

O lovely lonely lucid hours
When thought swings up to its full powers

. . . .

Such godhead humors are assured
To the reasonably matured;
Such dexterities defensive,
Pleasures brief but so intensive

. . . .

Boys, methought we did God's bidding
(Which I really mean, no kidding).
Caroled in my long hot bath,
Sang: Belike the time still hath
Foremath besides aftermath;
Sherlock Holmes the truth well put —
Watson, game is still afoot.

The Toulemonde poems represent Morley's attempt to express his own mature attitudes toward life in verse.

V   Translations from the Chinese

A much more important series of poems is Morley's large collection of Mandarin comments entitled "Translations from the Chinese." In the 1922 volume bearing that name, Morley explained how the Translations began as "Synthetic Poems," a "mild burlesque of the vers libre epidemic."[48] Furthermore, Morley felt "that free verse, then mainly employed as the vehicle of a rather gaudy impressionism or of mere eccentricity, might prove a viable medium for humorous, ironic, and satiric brevities. . . ."[49] The source of the "Chinese" persona for the poet was Arthur Waley's just-published translations, *170 Chinese Poems*, which Morley had read; from that volume he had learned about the humor and wisdom of real Chinese poets. The poetry of Witter Bynner *(The Beloved Stranger* [1919]) and Amy Lowell *(Fir-Flower Tablets [1921])* may also have influenced Morley, who knew both poets personally. Reacting to the new vogue of Oriental poetry, Morley commented "It was 'Loud sing Hokku' all across the map."[50]

Morley's early efforts were signed with a pseudonym, John Caven-
dish, and they were frequently attributed to a variety of mythical
Chinese poets, such as "No Sho," "O B'Oi," and "P'Ur Fish," but
Morley claimed that "Little by little my Chinese sages began to
coalesce and assume a voice of their own. I became not their creator
but their stenographer. I began to feel a certain respect and affection
for the 'Old Mandarin' who was dimly emerging as their Oriental
spokesman. . . . Of course he can be very annoying. It is maddening
to hear him contradict and ridicule the compromise and precious
makeshifts which we build for self-respect."[51]

The rationale behind the Old Mandarin's monologues is stated in
a "covering-poem" that is entitled "The Palimpsest":

> There is, in each man's heart,
> Chinese writing —
> A secret script, a cryptic language:
> The strange ideographs of the spirit,
> Scribbled over or half erased
> By the swift stenography of daily life.
>
> No man can easily decipher this cordiscript,
> This blurred text corrupted by fears and follies;
> But now and then,
> Reading his own heart
> (So little studied, such fine reading matter!)
> He sees fragments of rubric shine through —
> Old words of truth and trouble
> Illuminated, red and gold.
> The study of this hidden language
> Is what I call
> Translating from the Chinese.[52]

These Translations are wise, maliciously witty, charming, and imp-
ish. Pearl Buck, a writer with considerable Chinese experience,
wrote to Morley, "Of course, as you know, I have considered your
poems in the mandarin mood quite matchless, and I have never understood how it was an American or even an Occidental could write
them. After I met you, however, I divined in you a certain quality of
the mandarin, and then came to the conclusion that either you had
once been a mandarin in some previous life, or that the mandarin
quality, which I consider invaluable because it is both precious and
rare, is more universal than I thought."[53]

Despite the purported Chinese quality, however, Morley wrote in his memorandum book for September 12, 1945, that there was "never so *American* a book as the *Translations from the Chinese*." The Old Mandarin clearly reflected part of Christopher Morley's own character; in fact, "O.M." became one of his nicknames as he grew older. Thus it is less than remarkable that the Translations remained relatively consistent over the twenty-five years that Morley published them, varying little in style or content. They were popular enough to merit their own collections; following the original *Translations from the Chinese* volume in 1922, a revised edition with the same title appeared in 1927; *Mandarin in Manhattan*, in 1933; and *The Old Mandarin*, in 1947. In addition, a number of Translations were included in six other volumes of Morley's poetry, and in one collection of essays, as well.

Their subjects are, by and large, the same as other Morley works — life and literature, considered separately and together — but the unique "mandarin mood" which had attracted Pearl Buck's attention throws every subject into new perspective and subtly alters the meaning of the verses. Although the Translations were written throughout Morley's career, their tone contrasts sharply with that of his other poetry. While most Morley poems, such as those of the "Toulemonde" series, are characterized by a tone of earnestness and warmth, his Translations are distinguished by an inflection of objectivity, shrewdness and succinctness. For example, in a typical early Translation called "Only Word of Mouth," Morley displays this sharper, more skeptical tone:

> When I die
> I shall miss the ads.
> There will be plenty of ads in Heaven —
> Car-cards, billboards, double-page spreads,
> All the delightful old favorites,
> Such jolly folderol,
> Such appealing bunkum.
> But in Hell
> There will be no ads —
> It is too honest.[54]

Since the old Mandarin is, coincidentally, a poet, many of his utterances concern themselves with the fallible aspects of poetry, as in "The Cigarette Stub":

> Tossed aside in the uproar
> No Sho was quenched;
> But in his verses
> You will hear a satirical whisper
> Like the hiss of a cigarette stub
> Cast into a sink.[55]

Life is unmistakably woven into the Old Mandarin's literature.

The Old Mandarin was often impressed with curious aspects of American life and especially with American writers. Vachel Lindsay's youthful efforts to purchase his meals with poems won the O.M.'s admiration: "Here was a man with strong grasp of essentials!"[56] Walt Whitman is applauded for his "plausible philosophy/of indolence/Which, without soft concealments,/He called *Loafing*."[57] In "On Riverside Drive" the Old Mandarin is led to comment on the parallel between drifting ships at anchor and young writers:

> So quick they feel the changes
> In the currents of the time —
> Moored between
> The flood of E. M. Forster
> The ebb of Ezra Pound.[58]

Other writers than American ones drew the Old Mandarin's notice: "Grinding Teeth" quotes Lord Byron's dentist as saying that the poet's teeth were damaged from being ground together at night; he then remarks, "And I think how many Literary Critics/Are probably doing the same thing/This very night."[59] Two of the Translations deal with George Bernard Shaw, one of them entitled "G. B. S., 1856 —":

> What obsequies for dear old Shaw
> Who lived outside the canon law?
> Let's give him, to be truly Shavian,
> All rites, including Scandinavian.[60]

A quotation about Voltaire inspired the Translation entitled "Il Administre Sa Verve." Proving that there is poetry even in the law, the Old Mandarin cites Judge J. M. Woolsey's famous decision about Joyce's *Ulysses*: "In respect of the recurrent emergence of

the theme of sex, it must always be remembered that his locale was
Celtic and his season spring"; Morley then proceeds to convert that
statement into a poem:

> He heard the clock its knell tick
>   He heard the blackbird sing:
> Reaction peristaltic
>   And psychic too, they bring,
> For his locale was Celtic
>   And his season, spring.[61]

"Consolation for Commuters," one of Morley's last Translations,
attempts to apply the philosophy of Montaigne to a problem
typically faced by the commuting public:

> Michel de Montaigne
> Wouldn't mind if he missed a train.
> He'd simply say, Oh hell,
> The next one will do just as well.[62]

More often, however, the Old Mandarin used the Translations as
vehicles for his comments about literature and poetry. One of the
earliest of these is called "Bivalves":

> The pearl
> Is a disease of the oyster.
> A poem
> Is a disease of the spirit
> Caused by the irritation
> Of a granule of Truth
> Fallen into that soft gray bivalve
> We call the mind.[63]

"Irreverence" includes the character Poo Pitty Sing, the O. M.'s
favorite (and very feminine) pupil:

> Listen! (exclaimed the guests,
> Taking tea in the next room)
> Listen to the Old Mandarin's typewriter!
> He must be going good.
>
> Cumquats, said Poo Pitty Sing.
> When he goes as fast as that
> He's only X-ing out.[64]

The Translations sometimes rhyme, sometimes not, depending on the mood of the translator; "Stop-Short" doesn't bother with rhyme:

> All poems, in all tongues, in all ages,
> Say always the same thing:
> *Here am I, darling,*
> *But where art thou?*[65]

The "Bauble For Critics," however, depends on its tightly constructed form and rhyme:

> I am weary
> Of critical theory.
>
> I'm empiric
> About a lyric.
>
> Either it sings
> Like a happy peasant,
> Or — one of those things —
> It just doesn't.[66]

Many of the Translations speak incisively and cleverly about the vicissitudes of writing; they discuss the distractions faced by the poet, the many ways in which life jumps out at him with ideas and compulsions, and the difficulties caused by publishers. Morley used these little poems both as platforms for his ideas and as devices for self-criticism, but he was always mocking his own pretensions as a writer:

> Pray always to remain
> An unrecognized poet.
> Besides, this is a prayer
> Not unlikely to be fulfilled.[67]

At the same time, the alter-ego Old Mandarin was able to defend Morley (and writers, in general) more enthusiastically than a normal poetic voice would allow, as in the "Apology to Neighbors For Looking So Idle":

> The poet, on his verse intent,
>   Or the artist, dreaming paint,
> Probably look indolent —
>   But they ain't.[68]

Few of the Translations are visibly sentimental or personal since mandarins tend to conceal their more vulnerable emotions. However, in one poem which he later published as a Translation, but which was written for his Preface to *Bartlett's Familiar Quotations*, Morley spoke very directly from the heart; it is perhaps his most eloquent comment on poetry:

> In poetry there is one test of art:
> With whispering stealth, and keeping delicate time,
> It creeps into your mind; you find it there.
> You are my poem, then, for in my heart
> Lovelier than a sonnet you made rhyme
> And I had memorized you unaware.[69]

Unless poems work their way into real life, says Morley, they have little value. It is typical of his career that this very delicate work was written to accompany a witty and scholarly essay on language, itself the preface to a collection of other men's words and writings, arranged and selected by Morley.

VI *Final Thoughts*

Morley's poems range from the unabashedly sentimental to the caustically ironic, but he took his poetry, and the poems of others whom he tweaked or praised, very seriously. That he was a conscientious craftsman is demonstrated by the number of revisions he made in each of his poems and by the time he spent in choosing the vocabularly he employed. Surviving manuscripts of many of his poems indicate the care Morley took in their composition. "The Ballad of New York, New York," for example, exists in extensive autograph notes, one autograph manuscript, and four separate typescripts, three with additional manuscript notations. Diary entries indicate that Morley was anxiously brooding about the poem as early as July 30, 1944. On October 15 he made some notes for it; on October 17 he "worked all day, 10 a.m. until 1 a.m. next morning, in a joy of concentration" on the poem, only pausing one hour — to chop wood; otherwise, Morley "didn't eat or any other diversion except a few slugs of gin." On October 19 he worked all day revising the poem before sending it to an agent. Unable to place it, the agent returned the ballad, which Morley apparently put aside for some time. In July of the following year he made more revisions; proofs were sent to the author late in August from *The American Mercury;* and, after some additional revision, it was printed in October, 1945, and then reprinted in *Spirit Level*.

In the course of his revisions Morley altered the obscure description of a railway train from "bullgine 33" to "Number 33"; revised the dialect expression "a town of mickle price" to the more easily understood "that has no ceiling price"; and changed "the carlin witch" to "the old Belittlin' Witch." A letter to his editor, however, illustrates Morley's devotion to his craft and artistic integrity: "I have taken out all the words you think might puzzle readers — with the exception of the noble word *mappamond* which I would fight for to the end! It is a glorious word that hasn't been used since I don't know when, and I think the context shows its meaning clearly." "The Ballad of New York, New York" was one of Morley's favorites among his own poems, and it was inspired by the great amounts of time he had spent in the city. His decision to use the style of the old Border Ballad probably resulted from the time he had spent studying the ballad form while at Haverford under Francis B. Gummere, a noted scholar of the form. Morley was so proud of the completed poem that he confided to a friend "I truly think, I would rather have written Ballad of NYNY than The Waste Land."[70]

The opening of the poem transmits some of the feeling of the long (one-hundred twenty lines) ballad:

> Around the bend of Harbor Hill
> Comes Number 33,
> Says: Board the cars, my bonny boy,
> And ride to Town with me.
>
> A Town that has no ceiling price,
> A Town of double-talk;
> A Town so big men name her twice,
> Like so: N'Yawk, N'Yawk.[71]

Although Morley was able to remark lightly that there exists "a tacit understanding among civilized people that anything can be said in poetry, and it does not matter, because nobody is going to do anything about it,"[72] he felt deeply the potential of poems to sway emotions, revive tired spirits, or express a man's "private meditation."[73] Thus when Morley became active in the Fight For Freedom movement that urged American entry into World War II, he also began writing poems with a martial tone. "Fluctuat Nec Mergitur" was written in June, 1940, to commemorate the occupation of France; "The Spoken Word" appeared in December, 1942, in honor of the Battle of Stalingrad; but Morley's best-known war poem is "Around the Clock," addressed to the German people. A

long poem, it changes in style from terse verses filled with hard, tight
rhymes, to long, almost lyrical and alliterative lines, as some representative stanzas indicate:

> Sickness of heart,
>   Cold rains that sting —
> The time is short
>   Till fatal spring.
>
> Speak unreckoned,
>   Without revise:
> Every second
>   Someone dies.
>
>   .   .   .   .   .   .
>
> Germans, I tell you frank and fair,
> There is only one word.
>   The word *Despair*.
>
>   .   .   .   .
>
> Run, panic word, in every German mind:
> Poison the weary nerve and speed the sickness.
> After the frenzy comes the horrible weakness.
> Who says you this word *Despair?*
> It greets you from behind,
> But you look and there's no one there.
>
>   .   .   .   .
>
> The speed of a word in flight
>   All other speed can mock:
> Worse than bombing day-and-night
>   Is the Word-Around-the-Clock.
>
>   .   .   .   .
>
> We have drawn the sword
>   For a Peace to trust;
> It will be hard
>   But also just.
>
> It is not to be had
>   By wish devout;
> Peace has got to be
>   Sweated out.

You who have seen
 What men can bear,
Come; come clean;
 But first, *Despair*.[74]

Near the end of his career Morley used verse in "All Passion and
Publicity Spent" to express his reaction to his declining notoriety:

All passion spent, and all publicity,
My telephone not numbered in the book,
Nowhere will you find a happier man.
All birds are redbreast in the setting sun.[75]

Christopher Morley's poetry was, in his opinion, praised too
heavily in his youth but neglected in his maturity.[76] Most of it is
hardly great verse, but it is decidedly good poetry that is often very
beautiful. Because Morley's lyric gifts contested with his tendency
toward puns and humor, he created some excellent light verse in the
process. Morley evidently enjoyed writing poems; late in his career
as a writer he stated that "In the felicity of not writing by duress any
more, a grown man puts some of his private meditations into verse; a
good deal of which he has no intention of publishing."[77] This statement is not an assertion of "L'art pour l'art," but a declaration that
poetry was part of Morley's life — a reflection of an inner need —
more than a livelihood. That poetry was not sacred, or removed from
his other work, Morley demonstrated by including many of his
poems in volumes of essays, in novels, and even in newspaper
columns. Poetry, for Christopher Morley, was a special way of speaking which focused the art spirit on life; it fulfilled the one and en-
riched the other.

CHAPTER 5

Conclusions

I *Escaping Into Print*

IT was asserted earlier that Christopher Morley deliberately
concealed his deeper purposes in many of his essays — that he
used his practiced style and wit to hide from his casual readers the
serious tasks he often undertook in his writing. Thus it is less than
surprising that the clearest statement of Morley's goals and literary
philosophy appears in *Ex Libris Carissimis*, a book which was not
written at all, but spoken. This volume collects the five talks that
Morley delivered to the students of the University of Pennsylvania in
1931 as the first Rosenbach Fellow in Bibliography. The lectures
were published by the University of Pennsylvania Press, as well as by
the Oxford University Press; they even reappeared in a paperback
edition. Delivered without notes,[1] the talks were simply Christopher
Morley discussing his favorite subject, books, and how they come to
be.

Morley filled these lectures with anecdotes about particular books
and authors of importance to him, noting that, "my interest in bibliography is chiefly in its human overtones."[2] While bibliographers, in
general, value copies of books that have been signed or annotated by
the author, or that relate to some special incident in the writer's life,
Morley insisted that "we readers have our own associations which
are probably more important to us than the distant associations of
the authors."[3] He attempted in his talks to "trace the spiritual
genealogy"[4] of the books that he loved, trying to discover "By what
strangely delayed and twisted approaches have we come upon the
books that mean most to us?"[5] Although book collectors pay a
premium for books with the pages still uncut, Morley commented
that

An unopened copy of a book is to me a dead thing, or a thing that has never
been born. I like a book to show signs of life and use. Literature, to me, is a

110

form of companionship, and just as we do not love our friends any less because they may have a darn in their shirts or a crack in their shoes, or a crumple in their suits, similarly I like a book to show signs of life and usage, signs of reasonable wear, if not of tear. As I say, unopened copies over which many collectors go into ecstasies are to me something that has not yet been born. A book isn't born until someone reads it.[6]

As Morley frequently insisted, "books are intended to be read."[7]

There was a larger rationale behind Morley's belief in the personalization of literature; he adopted the phrase "escaped into print" to express his view of books:

We have to remind ourselves frequently that printed literature is an actual, living entity, emanating from the joys and agonies and perplexities of human beings. Too often, in reading textbooks about literature, one might imagine that writers have lived only for the purpose of writing and publishing. You might think that Oliver Goldsmith's only purpose in life was to write *She Stoops To Conquer*, or that O. Henry's extraordinary and tragic career had been totally expressed in a dozen volumes of ingenious and melodramatic short stories. We have to remind ourselves, I say, that the writings of the most admired and cherished authors are only a small "escape into print," only a fraction of the complete energy of those lives. Those printed relics that we love are only, we might say, what spilled over the brim as they carried the bowl of consciousness, sometimes with very unsteady hands, across the crowded places of life. And sometimes it is our duty and often our privilege to try to extend the area of those printed escapes by going around behind the textual record.[8]

This conception of books as the tip of the iceberg, as only small "escapes into print" of the lives of writers, is crucial to Christopher Morley's philosophy of writing. More importantly, it is central to an understanding of his career as a writer. Morley did not believe that exploration of the lives of authors was irrelevant either to books or to their readers: "I don't want you to think that casual memoranda, marginalia of that sort, are unworthy of the dignity of literature. That is the way that books are born and are made, and the inside history from the beginning and until the end will always be like that."[9] Books are made by people and they depend on people for their existences. Even the finest books in the world mean nothing without readers who understand and appreciate them; Morley reiterates that "the great things need our help."[10]

This special passion of Morley's was recognized by others in the literary world; Clifton Fadiman, discussing Morley's response to the written word, wrote that "When we say that Chris Morley loved books, we do not seem to be saying anything very striking. But he loved books in a peculiar valuable way. He saw them, as perhaps not all of our more learned contemporary men of letters always see them, as concretions of life. . . . His life — so busy, so varied, so filled with the kind of gusto today considered quaint — was in large measure dedicated to charging more leaden spirits than his own with the electricity that flows through good words by good writers."[11]

II *Collaboration by the Reader*

One of Morley's main contributions as an enthusiast of literature was his emphasis on the need for the reader to collaborate with the author. Morley encouraged his readers to think for themselves; in "A Letter to a Reader," written for an edition of Shakespeare, Morley claimed that he was writing "not an Introduction to Shakespeare, but an Introduction to Yourself-as-a-Reader-of-Shakespeare." Discussing Shakespeare's sonnets, Morley insisted, "don't worry about what Shakespeare may have meant, but what the Sonnets mean to YOU." To demonstrate the sort of collaboration that he believed essential, Morley drew on one of his favorite Shakespearean works, *The Tempest:* "When for instance you see in the line 'your swords are not too massy for your strengths' not merely Aries magicking the roughnecks, but a comment on our mechanized and militarized civilization, then you have collaborated with Shakespeare; you have brought him home to your present business and bosom; you have put your own exponent above his figure, and raised it to a higher power."

Insisting that he did not mean to praise ignorance, that careful study of an author's life and times is also necessary for a full appreciation of his work, Morley tried to encourage readers to collaborate. He believed that "the richest revenue of any art is the unearned increment it sometimes acquires from what happens later, of which the artist could have no specific foreboding." This illustrates one reason why Morley found *The Tempest* so important during World War II that he spent months working on an adaptation which he called *Tempest 1941*. In shortening the play, rearranging passages, and adding portions from other Shakespearean plays, Morley carried his philosophy of collaboration into the realm of re-creation. His vision of the play was a "political fugue," casting the passengers of the ship as "a group of fascist aristocrats who swarm up on deck as soon as the ship is in danger and get in the way of the crew." Caliban becomes a counterpart to Mussolini; Sycorax approximates Hitler; and Prospero, who personifies "Science, or Democracy, or Uncle Sam, or Thought itself," is, of course, opposed to Hitler and Mussolini. Morley was aware of the possible objections to this method of rewriting great literature, and he attempted a defense of what he had done through the mouth of Uncle Dan in *Thorofare*, a contemporaneous work. When Uncle Dan prepares an imaginative lecture on *The Tempest* along the lines of Morley's version of the play, a student objects, "You're making something out of it that the author couldn't possibly have Had in Mind." Echoing Morley's own sentiments, Dan retorts, "Why not? Isn't that the glory of literature?" This collaboration by Morley extended to other Shakespearean works at various points in Morley's career; he wrote a Second Scene for Act IV of *As You Like It* and a "wooing song" for Sir Toby in *Twelfth Night*.

Such collaboration between the reader and the author appeared as a Morley theme in many other essays and public addresses. One example of the benefits that he claimed for this type of imaginative reading can be found in a Morley talk at Adelphi College on March 7, 1939:

Sir Edmund Chambers says that Shakespeare lists a certain lady as one of the characters in a certain scene, and then that lady doesn't have anything to say. Edmund Chambers has been spending nights with Shakespeare for fifty years, and he said Shakespeare forgot and didn't give that woman anything to say. If he'd tried to act it (the scene is in *Measure for Measure*) . . . the scene where she is on the stage and has nothing to say. . . . Why does she have nothing to say? She has nothing to say because her lover is being dragged across the stage to be taken to prison, and she is choked with tears. Shakespeare took it for granted that no one expected her to talk. . . .

Morley did not so much expect his readers to rewrite the books they read as to rethink them when necessary, or at least to think themselves into the books. Perhaps with tongue in cheek, Morley suggested to Henry Seidel Canby, his *Saturday Review* associate, that Whitman's poem "To a Locomotive in Winter" was meant to symbolize the visits of Mrs. Anne Gilchrist, an English woman who travelled to Philadelphia ("every hormone on end" is the way Morley expressed it[12]) to comfort Walt. Canby, who took the idea seriously, later remarked in *Walt Whitman, an American* (1943) that "the guess is not out of the way, for Whitman was a symbolist long before this poem was written. . . ." On another occasion, Morley —

after seeing Ben Jonson's epitaph, "O rare Ben Jonson," cut into the
actual stone and noting the small space between the *O* and the *rare*
— was struck by the possibility of a pun on the Latin *ora e*, which
means "to pray." When Morley published this thesis in a small,
privately printed pamphlet, *My One Contribution to Seventeenth
Century Scholarship* (1927), a number of letters to the editor, both
pro and con, appeared in various publications. Even though no proof
for Morley's proposition was uncovered, he remarked that he was
still "not convinced that it may not have happened so, either by intent or by the accident of an unlettered stonecutter."

One of the ways Morley felt that readers could collaborate with
authors was to discover what they could about that part of the
author's life that did not "escape into print." "Find out what
problems of personality, circumstances, or joy, or sorrow," he ad-
vised, "caused and liberated and conditioned his professional
work."[13] While writing a preface for Boswell's *London Journal*,
Morley demonstrated this philosophy, working three months on the
piece, and producing a twenty-one-page document — although, as
published, the work is considerably shortened. In it, Morley
describes the physical characteristics of the author he believed to
have created "the greatest of all biographies outside Holy Writ"
with words that actually revealed much insight into the details of
Boswell's life: "the flat tip of the inquisitive trowel-nose — a com-
edian's nose — the pursed lips with their exquisite sense of relish, of
savouring and tasting; and the ears a little flanged, for sharp listen-
ing. The intellectual arched brows, the luxurious double chin, the
juridical crossed arms; and in the joy of tavern-talk all stewing and
steaming horror within well and truly forgotten — that is our
Boswell."

III   *The Artistic Mediator*

Morley's works — poetry, novels, essays, plays — are themselves
the "escape into print" of a remarkable man; his career was far more
than the sum of his publications. What is unique about Morley is his
enthusiastic acceptance of any role that promised to advance life by
aiding art — by making himself a conscious handmaiden or
"mediator"[14] between literature and the lives of real people.
Whether he accomplished this end by promoting the works he loved
or by acting as his own "purveyor of truth"[15] in his own writing was,
to him, of small importance. Whether acting as a kind of literary un-
derground railway conductor or "escaping into print" himself,

Christopher Morley was working toward the same end: bringing literature into people's lives.

Morley's view of his place in the world of letters was thus as pragmatic as his social philosophy, for he was concerned above all with the quality of life enjoyed by his fellow human beings. His writing was not meant as a channel for social dogma, but rather, at least partially, as an aid in escaping from the frustrations of life. The cohesiveness and stable quality of Morley's vision of society — benevolent, tolerant, and occasionally skeptical — freed him from the sort of philosophical crises which, while they may produce masterpieces in some cases, often restrict a writer's ability to create for substantial periods of time. Christopher Morley's messages were not subject to constant reevaluation; they were constant and serviceable. This unusual social vision is at once a limitation on Morley's ability to achieve greatness and an explanation of his prolific and professional output. Literature had a constant and valued place in his universe: it was a god served by writing, and Morley served it well and often.

In a lecture late in his career Morley told the story of the way in which gooseberry bushes had acted as the intermediaries for a pine-tree blight, describing the bushes' role as "like myself and teachers and amateur critics and people who like to think and talk about literature."[16] This pragmatism extended beyond his essays and talks into Morley's novels and poems: the lovely poem entitled "VIII" brought the issue to a very personal level:

> No bird has built an April nest
>   More instinctive than my rhyme,
> A hidden coil where thought can rest
>   In lonely or in stormy time.
>
> I weave for you these twigs and straws,
>   The casual shreds of every day:
> Your love can shelter there for pause
>   And, when it needs to, fly away.
>
> I built it hidden, shy, unknown,
>   And weatherwise, with simple care.
> And even when the bird has flown
>   The empty nest will still be there.[17]

Quite early in his career Christopher Morley outlined his conception of the social role of literature:

The poet performs the greatest of social functions: he elucidates the secrets of other hearts by eavesdropping at his own. At the bottom of almost every heart is terror. But it comforts men to know that others are also afraid. It is because we hardly know what we ourselves think that we are endlessly eager to know the thoughts of others. The poets discover us to ourselves; and they speak not apprehensively, not embarrassed, not beshrewed and distracted by a muddle of affairs, but in that perfection of power and happiness that comes of impassioned solitude. By making us share their sufferings they have eased themselves, and eased us, too.[18]

In order to be relevant to life, Morley believed, literature has to speak to people's most deeply felt needs: "It is chiefly in the emergencies of life that you discover what literature is really most helpful. Suppose you are reading to someone in a hospital, would you choose *Ulysses?* I doubt it."[19]

    This attitude does not connote any disapproval of experimental writing or even of *Ulysses*. Rather, Morley was convinced that, at certain times in their lives, people need different things from literature, which is useless if it cannot supply those needs — the same message he had spread in *Parnassus on Wheels*. If the beauty that he perceived in life could be transmitted to another human being, could be made real to someone who needed that beauty, then Morley felt that he had succeeded; as he put it in "Two Sonnets to Themselves,"

> Since you are wise and generous and kind
> I tell you this. I tell it to you only,
> But I am proud that others too may find
> Our beauty serviceable when they're lonely.[20]

Morley set out a measure for any work of art or literature: "Does it really accomplish the purpose it sets out to do, whether in great matters or small? If a thing accomplishes its purpose then it is perfect of its kind."[21] The general purpose that Christopher Morley assigned to literature, and to his participation in the universe of literature, was the promotion of life in all of its variety and beauty.

IV   *Morley's Literary Status*

When, in 1934, Doubleday, Doran and Company issued a volume of what it believed to be "Great Autobiography," it included a small Christopher Morley essay entitled "The Autogenesis of a Poet," as well as autobiographical works of Walt Whitman, Joseph Conrad, and Helen Keller. The publishers noted of Morley that "Almost since he waked to a consciousness of the world, he has felt so urgently the infinite mystery and beauty and fun of living that he has been under compulsion to write and talk about it."[22] Not only did Morley find this beauty in the episodes and emotions of his own life but in the literature of others as well. When he felt some particular joy in a new way, Morley wrote about it; when he found it in the writings of others, Morley wrote about his discovery with fervor, hoping thereby to bring that beauty to people who needed it in whatever way he could.

Christopher Morley was a man intoxicated with literature as the distilled brandy of life. It is thus difficult to appraise him intelligently solely as a poet, a novelist, an essayist, a publicist, a bookseller, or a theatrical promoter. Morley integrated all of these roles into a coherent, meaningful whole; he was a man who truly "made friends with himself." This multiplicity of literary roles was recognized by other writers and critics; Vincent Starrett spoke of Morley as "the only writer I have ever known who seemed to me to fulfill the role of man of letters with the humor and dignity of a great tradition."[23]

A more detailed consideration of Morley's unique position in the American literary world comes from the pen of the well-known novelist, John P. Marquand:

I shall always think of Chris Morley when someone in the literary world refers to someone else as a 'man of letters.' I shall think of him with affection and respect because, if I had not been a friend of his, I would never have known what 'man of letters' really meant. Unless I think of Chris today, the term still confuses me. Perhaps in the distant past—shall we say in the Edwardian era—the man of letters may have been a member of a well-known genus, but not after World War I, and surely not after World War II. It seems to me that in my lifetime the man-of-letters species has grown as extinct as the whooping crane, but this unhappy contingency has not occurred because lots of people have not wanted or tried to be men of letters. The universities are full of them and they proliferate even into the protected areas of the hard-bitten literary world. Yet judging from the one I have known, they are pretenders when compared to Christopher Morley. Due perhaps to my provincial background, he is the only man I have ever known who might in the best tradition be called a man of letters. . . .

. . . I find myself still wondering as I write what the term in its entirety implies. A man of letters must obviously possess a wide knowledge of literature and be imbued with special literary enthusiasms. A man of letters should also be able to perform in different literary fields with marked distinction—in verse, in the essay and in fiction. Christopher Morley could move effortlessly in these, and so, too, could many others I have known, but all of them except Chris Morley have possessed aggressive intellectual pretensions. He, of all the writers I have known, had something that raised him above the contenders, something that enabled him to write *Where the Blue Begins* and *Thunder on the Left.* I dislike to paraphrase, but I, venture to paraphrase Harold Bell Wright in the beginning of one of his most popular novels. "A man of letters," Harold Bell Wright might have written, "to be a man of letters must be a man." The truth is most of the sedulous men of letters I have known do not meet this standard, but Christopher Morley did.

It is very easy to carry the process of definition a step further. Christopher Morley is the only man of letters I can accept because he did not know he was one, and furthermore, if he had been told, he would not have cared.[24]

When Morley died, he instructed his executors to publish the following message in *The New York Times* and in *The New York Herald Tribune:*

> Christopher Morley, who died March 28, 1957,
> asked his executors to use this space
> "To send my unchanged love to many kind and
> forbearing friends. Our good adventures and
> absurdities were not forgotten, nor occasions
> of beauty and moments of disgust. Specially
> I wanted to apologize for so many unanswered
> letters through so many years. Their messages,
> of whatever sort, were often in mind.
> I had many reasons for gratitude,
> and I was grateful."[25]

It seems very likely that Christopher Morley felt that he had accomplished many of the tasks he had set himself—that, in his own terms and by his own standards, he was a success. While his popularity waned in his later years, Morley does not seem to have hungered for additional recognition. In his last volume of essays, for example, Morley notes that he had been elected to the National Institute of Arts and Letters but that be had never bothered to attend a meeting.[26] He was relatively prosperous, widely read, and surrounded with his family and friends of many years' standing. Morley thus stands in sharp contrast to his close friend Don Marquis, who died alone, embittered, and financially insecure. Marquis, after years of struggling to write, thought of himself as a failure, but Christopher Morley was, apparently, comfortable with his writing and with his other pursuits to the end of his life.

Since so much of his career was writing, much of which he evidently felt succeeded according to the goals he had set for it, Morley might have been unlikely to predict the low level of interest in his work after his death. Many of the factors that have contributed to Morley's lack of recent popularity, however, are easy to select: his essays are heavily topical, and were most widely published in ephemeral journals; much of his poetry is very traditional in form, and consequently of little interest to modern poets who are preoccupied with innovation and experiment; many of his novels are too bookish to appeal to a large audience and they, too, often suffer from a dated appearance. Although these reasons may be valid, they are not entirely persuasive. Many of Morley's essays are superbly written, and they concern some of the high points of American literary and social culture in the first half of the twentieth century. The impressively large corpus of essays which Christopher Morley left treats most of the important and many of the more interestingly obscure figures in American literature of that period, especially those who were centered in New York City.

While much of Morley's poetry is traditional in appearance, his "Translations from the Chinese" are both unique and innovative. Many of his other poems have found their ways into anthologies. In fact, the publication in 1965 of *Bright Cages*, an anthology of some of Christopher Morley's finest poems, may mark a revival of interest in his poetry, as the publication in 1970 of a collection of his essays, *Prefaces Without Books*, denotes new interest in that portion of Morley's writing. Although Christopher Morley may never achieve recognition as more than, in his own words, "one more minor poet,"[27] he was a good poet who left much worth remembering.

The many novels that Christopher Morley wrote are the most difficult of all his work to evaluate today. Some of them are obviously trivial works and are of concern only to Morley collectors. Others, such as *Human Being* and *Thorofare*, suffered even at publication from the overindulgence of Morley's proclivity for using novels as literary pulpits, although this quality is more damaging in *Thorofare* than in the other novel. The insistent reiteration of Morley's theme that literature is tied irretrievably to life often becomes obtrusive and makes these works remote from the average reader. *The Man Who Made Friends With Himself* is a special case, a rare gem of great interest only to bibliophiles and to Morleyites but, in Morley's words, "perfect of its kind."[28] *Where the Blue Begins* and *Thunder on the Left* were popular novels when they appeared, and both seem to have fared quite well during the last fifty years. *Where the Blue*

Begins is probably too fanciful, except as a children's book, for circulation today; but *Thunder on the Left* shows few signs of obsolescence, either in style or in content. While not masterpieces, both are finely crafted works that have some potential for future recognition.

Morley's best chances for a permanent readership seem to rest on the rather atypical *Kitty Foyle*, however. In shifting the balance away from the promotional and literary, and toward the personal and social, Morley temporarily transcended the limitations that he placed upon himself in many of his other novels. Written with the skill and seriousness that are characteristic of all of Christopher Morley's novels, *Kitty Foyle* abandons to a large extent the Morley mission of bringing great literature to the attention of the common man and, paradoxically, in doing so Morley comes closest to having produced great literature. *Kitty Foyle* is a book that is representative of American life in the 1930's; it is concerned with the problems of the day; it has excellent prose and an entertaining style; and it may well become one of the notable social and literary documents produced in its era.

Christopher Morley's chances for recognition by posterity make an intriguing subject for speculation, but such chance is by no means the measure of the man. The search for fame and for a perpetual readership were simply not the main forces that motivated Christopher Morley. His mission which he defined as early as *Parnassus on Wheels* was to help bring beauty and great literature to those people alive in America during his own lifetime. Morley, who worried about the quality of American civilization and about the future of literature in it, noted in the mid-1930's: "Now the concern that occupies my own mind is that probably never anywhere, at any time, was secluded or creative thinking so difficult to achieve as in America today."[29] In his writing, in his publicizing of his theatrical promotions, and in his editorial involvements, Christopher Morley tried to foster those conditions of reflection and contemplation which he believed lacking in his society.

Christopher Morley was a professional writer, but he was not just a writer. His true profession was literature in all its manifestations in American society. As a complete literary man, Morley committed himself to institutions that he believed likely to foster the development of American literature, such as *The Saturday Review* and the Book-of-the-Month Club. Morley's role in the club is illustrative: his membership on its executive board enabled him to advance the careers of those authors who, he felt, deserved wider exposure; and his frequent book reviews for the club's publication gave him an opportunity to speak to a large reading public about his literary concerns. His "Trade Winds" column in *The Saturday Review* was created to provide a forum for literary news, for the details of literary life which Morley believed so essential to an understanding of literature; the fact that the column has remained in existence since Morley ceased to write it attests both to the need it filled and to Morley's success in establishing it. The success of *The Saturday Review* itself was partly attributable to Morley's columns and to his editorial contributions.

In Morley's very first job with Doubleday, he fought successfully for the publication of William McFee's *Casuals of the Sea*. Later in his career, as he accumulated more and more influence in American publishing circles, Morley was frequently able to act as mediator between books which he felt needed circulation and publishers who were wary of them. In *Ex Libris Carissimis* Morley notes two of these instances, the cases of C. E. Montague's *Disenchantment* and of Rupert Brooke's *1914 and Other Poems*.[30] Each of these books, interestingly enough, had been published in England but ignored in America until Morley was alerted to them and began to work for their publication. These examples are extreme cases of Morley's mediating and publicizing activity which, however, continued on a lesser plane throughout his lifetime. The attention paid to the fiction of Joseph Conrad and to the prose of Walt Whitman today is very much the result of Christopher Morley's labor.

While not a writer of the first rank, Christopher Morley was a literary figure of major importance; for, to use his own formulation, only part of his life "escaped into print." His prolific career as a writer was encompassed by an all-embracing involvement in literature, an involvement which included everything from printing books to creating an environment favorable to their composition. Few men have been so pervasive in the world of American letters, or so influential in shaping the literary interests of their times. It would be a mistake, however, to allow the unique breadth of Morley's career to obscure the high quality of the writing that he produced. A writer who often won high critical acclaim, as well as a large popular readership, Morley left his mark on American literature as a writer, as well as a "literary man." The experiments he pursued, such as those in *The Trojan Horse* and in the "Translations from the Chinese," may not have founded new schools of writing, but they were no less innovative and stimulating to readers of their day for that. The social documents Morley created, such as *History of an Autumn* and *Kitty Foyle,* were not so sensational as some of the "realism" of his contemporaries, but they may well provide a more understanding and a more insightful portrait of twentieth-century America for just that reason.

Christopher Morley's contribution to American literature must, therefore, be measured both by the books he produced and by the valuable services he rendered to all books. When he first built his writing studio, The Knothole, in his back yard, Morley selected an appropriate motto for himself. Over the door he carved a Latin slogan, drawn from a letter from Desiderius Erasmus to Bishop Fuller in 1524. It can still be read today on The Knothole, which stands in Christopher Morley Park on Long Island: "ASSIDVVS SIS IN BIBLIOTHECA OVAE TIBI PARADISI LOCO EST" (How Busy You Are in Your Library, Which is Your Paradise!).[31]

Notes and References

(Unless otherwise identified, manuscript material is from the Christopher Morley Collection at the Humanities Research Center at the University of Texas.)

Chapter One

1. This estimate was made by Peter Keisogloff, a Cleveland, Ohio, bookseller and a friend of Morley in a personal conversation with co-author Mark I. Wallach on January 15, 1971.
2. *Christopher Morley, His History* (Garden City, 1922), p. 7.
3. Jon Bracker, *Bright Cages* (Philadelphia, 1965), p. 13.
4. Helen Oakley, *Christopher Morley on Long Island* (Roslyn, 1967), p. 15.
5. R. Buckminster Fuller made this declaration in a personal conversation with co-author Mark I. Wallach at Wesleyan University, Middletown, Connecticut, on February 10, 1970.
6. Marquis's inscription can still be read in The Knothole in Christopher Morley Park on Long Island.
7. Helen Oakley, *Christopher Morley*, p. 14.
8. Walt Whitman, *Two Prefaces*, introduction by Christopher Morley (Garden City, 1926), p. xx.
9. *Born in a Beer Garden, or She Troupes to Conquer* (New York, 1930).
10. Ibid., p. 41.
11. Ibid., p. 31.
12. Bracker, *Bright Cages*, p. 28.
13. Oakley, *Christopher Morley*, p. 22.
14. Blythe Morley, *The Intemperate Season* (New York, 1948). The novel is an essentially juvenile romance.
15. *Internal Revenue* (Garden City, 1933), opening quotation.
16. This same quotation is used admiringly by Morley in *John Mistletoe* (New York, 1931), p. 394.

17. Guy R. Lyle and H. Tatnall Brown, Jr., *A Bibliography of Christopher Morley* (Washington, 1952), p. 3.

18. *Christopher Morley, His History* (Garden City, 1922), p. 8.

19. "Temperamental Writing," *Internal Revenue* (New York, 1933), p. 185.

20. *Modern Essays* (New York, 1921).

21. *Modern Essays for Schools* (New York, 1922).

22. *The Bowling Green* (Garden City, 1924).

23. *A Book of Days* (1930).

24. *Ex Libris* (Camden, 1936).

25. *Inward Ho!* (Garden City, 1923), p. 151.

26. *Ex Libris Carissimis* (Philadelphia, 1932), p. 131.

27. *Shandygaff* (Garden City, 1918), p. 61.

28. Ibid., p. 63.

29. *Streamlines* (Garden City, 1936), p. 130.

30. *The Romany Stain* (Garden City, 1926), p. 218.

31. *Hostages to Fortune* (Haverford, 1925), p. 106.

32. *Streamlines*, p. 107.

33. *Shandygaff*, p. 22.

34. Ibid., p. 27.

35. *The Romany Stain*, p. 245.

36. *The Ironing Board* (Garden City, 1949), p. 23.

37. *John Mistletoe* (Garden City, 1931), p. 141.

38. *Letters of Askance* (New York, 1939), p. 82.

39. Edward Anthony, *O Rare Don Marquis* (Garden City, 1962), p. 491.

40. Ibid., p. 360.

41. *Letters of Askance*, p. 110.

42. *The Ironing Board*, p. 183.

43. Walt Whitman, *Two Prefaces*, introduction by Christopher Morley (Garden City, 1926), p. xvii.

44. *Born in a Beer Garden* (New York, 1930), p. 90mf-   5$The Powder of Sympathy (Garden City, 1923), p. 153.

46. *Rudolph and Amina* (New York, 1930), pp. 67 & 146.

47. *The Ironing Board*, p. 169.

48. Guy R. Lyle and H. Tatnall Brown, Jr., *A Bibliography of Christopher Morley*, p. 45.

49. Ibid., p. 64.

50. *Colophon* (1930).

51. See Footnote 1, Chapter 1.

52. Anonymous, "In Memoriam Christopher Morley," (New York, 1957), p. 6.

53. This suggestion comes from a personal letter to co-author Mark I. Wallach by Helen Oakley, president of the Christopher Morley Knothole Association, dated February 7, 1971.

Chapter Two

1. *The Ironing Board* (Garden City, 1949), p. 12.

2. Ibid., "On Belonging to Clubs," p. 28.

3. *Ex Libris Carissimis* (Philadelphia, 1932), p. 45.

4. *Plum Pudding* (Garden City, 1922).

5. *Streamlines* (Garden City, 1936).

6. *Letters of Askance* (Philadelphia, 1939), p. 316.

7. *The Ironing Board.*

8. *A Bibliography of Christopher Morley*, (Washington, 1952), p. 139 ff.

9. This information is contained in a letter by Morley to Lillian Morley, June 23, 1923.

10. *Religio Journalistici* (Garden City, 1924), p. 11.

11. St. John Adcock, *The Glory That Was Grub Street* (New York, 1928), p. 239.

12. Walt Whitman, *Leaves of Grass*, introduction by Morley, p. vii.

13. *Shandygaff* p. 222.

14. Ibid., p. 223.

15. Ibid., p. 227.

16. *Streamlines*, p. 122.

17. *The Powder of Sympathy* (Garden City, 1923), p. 103.

18. Ibid., p. 106.

19. *Letters of Askance*, p. 45.

20. *The Romany Stain* (Garden City, 1926), p. 77.

21. Ibid., p. 183.

22. *Letters of Askance*, p. 169.

23. *Ex Libris Carissimis*, p. 69.

24. *Thorofare* (New York, 1942), p. 316.

25. *Inward Ho!* (Garden City, 1923), p. 70.

26. Lawrence Durrell, *The Spirit of Place* (New York, 1969).

27. *John Mistletoe* (Garden City, 1931), p. 3.

28. *The Romany Stain*, p. 251.

29. "Slip Cover," a brief autobiographical essay by Morley written for release by Doubleday and Company in 1949; the three-page mimeographed sheet was made available to co-author Jon Bracker by Louise Thomas of Doubleday.

30. Ibid.

31. *The Romany Stain*, p. 251.

32. *The Ironing Board*, p. 195.

33. *The Saturday Review of Literature*, (August 9, 1924), p. 29.

34. *The Powder of Sympathy*, p. 262.

35. *Shandygaff*, p. 166.

36. Ibid., p. 260.

37. "Dominion Over Experience," *Off the Deep End* (Garden City, 1928), p. 236.

38. *John Mistletoe*, p. 10.

39. There are further references by Morley to Smith's phrase. One occurs in "Passivity Program," an address given by Morley on March 7, 1939, at Adelphi College (and published by The Argus Book Shop, Chicago, that same year): ". . . there are people who, no matter how exciting their experiences, never rise above or aside those experiences to get an imaginative or synthetic purview of them." Another reference to the phrase is found in a memorandum book notation, September 20, 1942: "I come back again and again to LPS's touchstone: 'imag[inative] dominion over experience' — (wh[ich] I pursue Tues, Thurs and Sats!)." And in *The Man Who Made Friends With Himself* (New York, 1949), Richard Tolman thinks: "The important thing. Each single mind must somehow integrate and dominate its own experience."

40. "A Preface to the Profession of Journalism," *Plum Pudding* (Garden City, 1921), p. 52. Concerning the same subject, Morley copied into his memorandum book, September 2, 1934, Alexander Smith's remarks, from an essay in *Dreamthorp:* "The value of egotism depends entirely on the egotist. If the egotist is weak, his egotism is worthless. If the egotist is strong, acute, full of distinctive character, his egotism is precious, and remains a possession of the race."

41. "Iota Subscript," *Parson's Pleasure* (New York, 1923), p. 39.

42. Morley's interest in Watson's epigram can be gauged by the fact that he copied the lines into his memorandum book, March 25, 1922, and again — one line only — on February 22, 1923; he then quoted the poem in its entirety in *Inward Ho!* and in an essay, "Diary For Daughters," in *Streamlines*, where he quotes the verse from memory.

43. "Iota Subscript," *Parson's Pleasure*, p. 39.

44. "A Sample of Bran," *Streamlines*, p. 234, where it is quoted as "an extraordinary little paragraph."

45. *Hostages to Fortune* (Haverford, 1925), p. 10.

46. *The Powder of Sympathy*, p. 30.

47. *Letters of Askance*, p. 110.

48. Henry Seidel Canby, *American Estimates* (New York, 1929), p. 62.

49. *The Ironing Board*, p. 102.

50. Ibid.

51. *Streamlines*, p. 54.

52. Ibid., p. 66.

53. *Streamlines*, Dedication.

54. John McHale, *R. Buckminster Fuller* (New York, 1962), p. 17.

55. Frederick Lewis Allen, "History of an Autumn," *The Saturday Review of Literature*, XIX, 6 (December 3, 1938), p. 32.

56. Franklin D. Roosevelt, letter to Morley, December 21, 1938.

57. *History of an Autumn* (Philadelphia, 1938), p. 44.

58. *The Ironing Board*, p. 177.

Chapter Three

1. *John Mistletoe* (Garden City, 1931), p. 153.
2. *Parnassus on Wheels* (Garden City, 1917), p. 39.
3. Ibid., p. 79.
4. *The Haunted Bookshop* (Philadelphia, 1955), p. 17.
5. Ibid.
6. Ibid., p. 248.
7. According to an interview with Morley in the *Dayton Daily News*, March 30, 1936.
8. Letter from Morley to Vincent Starrett, November 16 (year not indicated on letter).
9. "Author's Note," *Where the Blue Begins: A Divine Comedy* (New York, 1925), p. 2.
10. *John Mistletoe*, p. 246.
11. Ibid., p. 154.
12. Letter from Morley to Felix Riesenberg, November 24, 1923; this is quoted in Felix Riesenberg's *Living Again* (New York, 1939), p. 324.
13. "Harry Dounce tells me," Morley noted in his journal, June 7, 1922, "that Puckette was very indignant over the theology of *Where the Blue Begins*, which seemed to him blasphemous in the extreme!"
14. *Where the Blue Begins* (Garden City, 1922), p. 24.
15. Ibid., p. 55.
16. Letter to Lillian Morley, June 22, 1922.
17. The story changed slightly in Morley's later retellings: in *The New York Times*, the story is told as follows:
Rudyard Kipling once said to me, strangely, "What a fool you were to write a book like that! How you'll regret it! Thank God I was never rash enough to try to write about the inside of things! Why did you do it?"
He looked at me very piercingly from under his extraordinary thatched eyebrows, and I could only say, with some embarrassment, "I had to."
His face changed. "Was it laid upon you? Don't say any more. I understand perfectly."
It was an odd thing for Kipling to say, for he, as much as any man in our lifetime, has suggested the insides of things.
When retold in *Letters of Rudyard Kipling*, the dialogue is recreated in this fashion: "Kipling asked, 'Why on earth did you write it?' When Morley explained that he had to, Kipling replied, 'Was it laid upon you? Ah, then I understand perfectly.' Then, after a pause he remarked, 'But how you will regret it. Thank Heaven, *I* never tried to write about the insides of things.' "
18. As quoted in an interview, *Cleveland Plain Dealer*, November 22, 1933.
19. *Thunder on the Left* (Garden City, 1925), p. 39.
20. Ibid. p. 118.
21. Ibid., p. 226.
22. As quoted in *The New York Times Book Review*, November 29, 1925.

23. "Blue Silk," *Off the Deep End* (Garden City, 1928,) p. 262.

24. "Mind Erosion," *Streamlines* (Garden City, 1936), p. 52.

25. *Human Being* (Garden City, 1932), p. vii.

26. Ibid., p. 18.

27. As quoted in *The Hartford Daily News*, December 10, 1935.

28. "Introduction," *Human Being* (New York, 1940), p. x.

29. Ibid.

30. From a letter to Frank Henry at Doubleday, Doran, which bears no date. The letter contains copy for the advertising campaign for the novel, and begins "One of the best of modern epigrams. . . ." (A copy of the letter was supplied to co-author Jon Bracker by Doubleday and Company).

31. *Human Being*, p. 36.

32. Ibid., p. 85.

33. Ibid., p. 91.

34. Ibid., p. 346.

35. *It's a Kind of a Memorabilia, A Letter About the Trojan Horse . . .* (Philadelphia, 1937), p. 4.

36. "Thoughts in a Dymaxion Car," *Streamlines*, p. 32.

37. "Mind Erosion," *Streamlines*, p. 32.

38. *It's a Kind of a Memorabilia*, p. 5.

39. *Inward Ho!* (Garden City, 1923), p. 14.

40. *Kitty Foyle* (New York, 1939), p. 280.

41. *The Middle Kingdom* (New York, 1944), p. 20.

42. Autograph note by Morley on typed, carbon copy, manuscript of excerpt from unpublished memoirs of Felix Morley, in the collection of H. Tatnall Brown, Jr. (The note was written some time after January, 1946, when the memoirs were begun.)

43. "Exceptionally beautiful day . . . ," a typed, carbon copy, manuscript note, no date, in the University of Texas Collection.

44. Dorothy Deegan, *The Stereotype of the Single Woman in American Novels* (New York, 1951), p. 167.

45. Letter to J. W. Lippincott, August 11, 1938; a note in Morley's handwriting indicates that the letter was never sent.

46. Theodore H. Mecke, Jr., "T. A. Daly Fights Filth Columnists," *The Queen's Work* (published in 1945 or 1944, according to the author, from whom further information is unavailable.)

47. As quoted by Frederick Woltman in an interview in the *New York World Telegram*, November 3, 1939.

48. Morley's letter to Martin Birnbaum, April 10, 1942.

49. Morley's letter to Harry Hansen, October 24, 1939.

50. Morley's letter to Ben Abramson, September 22, 1939.

51. Morley's letter to Frank Henry, October 10, 1939.

52. Morley's letter to A. E. Newton, July 10, 1940.

53. *Kitty Foyle*, p. 339.

54. Harry R. Warfel, *American Novelists of Today* (New York, 1951), p. 310.

55. "Notes on an Island," *The Ironing Board* (Garden City, 1949), p. 35.

56. "Today, I said to myself . . . ," typed manuscript notes, March 24, 1940.

57. Robert Van Gelder, "An Interview With Christopher Morley," *Writers and Writing* (New York, 1946), p. 336.

58. Ibid., p. 335.

59. *The Middle Kingdom*, p. 10.

60. Morley's letter to Daniel Longwell, July 28, 1948.

61. Morley's letter to Vincent Starrett, March 7, 1949 (in recipient's possession).

62. Morley's letter to Edward Weeks, January 20, 1951; the letter bears Morley's autograph note, "not sent."

63. Harvey Breit, "Talk With Christopher Morley," *The New York Times Book Review*, July 12, 1949, p. 13.

64. *The Ironing Board*, p. 175.

65. Morley's letter to Elizabeth Winspear, March 4, 1948 (in the possession of the recipient).

66. Morley's letter to Louise Thomas, September 19, 1948.

67. *The Man Who Made Friends With Himself* (Garden City, 1949), p. 12.

68. Ibid., p. 120.

69. Ibid., p. 50.

70. Ibid., p. 15.

71. Ibid., p. 17.

72. *The Middle Kingdom*, p. 5.

73. *The Man Who Made Friends With Himself*, p. 75.

74. Ibid., p. 126.

Chapter Four

1. *Spirit Level and Other Poems* (Cambridge, 1946), p. 32.

2. Bracker, *Bright Cages*, p. 13.

3. Ibid.

4. *Parson's Pleasure* (New York, 1923), p. 13.

5. *The Man Who Made Friends With Himself*, p. 18.

6. *The Middle Kingdom* (New York, 1944), back jacket notes.

7. *The Middle Kingdom*, p. 10.

8. "The Watchman's Sonnet," *The Middle Kingdom*, p. 18.

9. *Parson's Pleasure*, p. 100.

10. Elmer Adler, "The Eighth Sin," *Breaking into Print* (New York, 1937), p. 153.

11. Ibid., p. 155.

12. Bracker, *Bright Cages*, p. 22.

13. Ibid., p. 21.

14. *Chimneysmoke* (New York, 1921), p. 52.

15. Ibid., p. 28.

16. Ibid., p. 94.
17. Ibid., p. 100.
18. Ibid., p. 112.
19. *The Middle Kingdom,* back jacket notes.
20. *Chimneysmoke,* p. 144.
21. *The Middle Kingdom,* p. 17.
22. Ibid., p. 26.
23. *Spirit Level,* p. 31.
24. *The Middle Kingdom,* p. 7.
25. *Spirit Level,* p. 37.
26. Ibid., p. 29.
27. *Chimneysmoke,* p. 219.
28. Ibid., p. 179.
29. *Parson's Pleasure,* p. 81.
30. *Chimneysmoke,* p. 249.
31. *Parson's Pleasure,* p. 58, and *Poetry Package* (New York, 1950), no page number.
32. Morley's letter to William Rose Benét, May 16, 1949.
33. Harvey Breit, "Talk With Christopher Morley," *The New York Times Book Review,* June 12, 1949, p. 4.
34. *Gentlemen's Relish* (New York, 1955), p. 14.
35. *The Middle Kingdom,* p. 31.
36. *Chimneysmoke,* p. 86.
37. *The Middle Kingdom,* p. 18.
38. *Gentlemen's Relish,* p. 82.
39. *Chimneysmoke,* p. 98.
40. Ibid., p. 251.
41. *Gentlemen's Relish,* p. 45.
42. *The Middle Kingdom,* p. 3.
43. *Gentlemen's Relish,* p. 68.
44. Ibid., p. 39.
45. *Spirit Level,* p. 15.
46. *Chimneysmoke,* p. 204.
47. Ibid., p. 228.
48. *Translations from the Chinese* (New York, 1922), p. vii.
49. Ibid., p. viii.
50. Ibid.
51. Ibid., p. viii.
52. Ibid., p. 19.
53. Bracker, *Bright Cages,* p. 24.
54. *Translations from the Chinese,* p. 36.
55. Ibid., p. 52.
56. Ibid., p. 58.
57. Ibid., p. 59.
58. *The Middle Kingdom,* p. 86.

59. *Mandarin in Manhattan* (Garden City, 1933), p. 117.
60. *The Old Mandarin* (New York, 1947), p. 12.
61. *The Middle Kingdom*, p. 108.
62. *The Old Mandarin*, p. 61.
63. *Translations from the Chinese*, p. 77.
64. *The Old Mandarin*, p. 56.
65. *Mandarin in Manhattan*, p. 23.
66. *The Old Mandarin*, p. 6.
67. Ibid., p. 80.
68. Ibid., p. 108.
69. *The Middle Kingdom*, p. 90.
70. Morley's letter to Elizabeth B. Winspear, May 3, 1947 (in possession of the recipient).
71. *Spirit Level*, p. 7.
72. *Shakespeare and Hawaii* (Garden City, 1933), p. 54.
73. *The Ironing Board* (Garden City, 1949), p. 157.
74. *The Middle Kingdom*, p. 44.
75. Bracker, *Bright Cages*, p. 32.
76. Stanley J. Kunitz, *Twentieth Century Authors* (New York, 1955), p. 691.
77. *The Ironing Board*, p. 157.

Chapter Five

1. *Ex Libris Carissimis* (Philadelphia, 1932), p. vii.
2. Ibid., p. 26.
3. Ibid., p. 27.
4. Ibid.
5. Ibid.
6. Ibid., p. 9.
7. Ibid., p. 3.
8. Ibid., p. 46.
9. Ibid., p. 53.
10. Ibid., p. 68.
11. "In Memoriam Christopher Morley," p. 3.
12. "The Atom Splitter," *The Ironing Board* (Garden City, 1949), p. 180.
13. *Shakespeare and Hawaii*, p. 44.
14. *Ex Libris Carissimis*, p. 54.
15. Ibid., p. 129.
16. *Shakespeare and Hawaii*, p. 50.
17. *The Middle Kingdom*, (New York, 1944), p. 11.
18. *Inward Ho!* (Garden City, 1923), p. 19.
19. *The Romany Stain* (Garden City, 1926), p. 80.
20. *The Middle Kingdom*, p. 20.
21. *Shakespeare and Hawaii*, p. 40.

22. *A Book of Great Autobiography* (Garden City, 1934), publisher's note.
23. Letter to co-author Jon Bracker, February 8, 1964.
24. "In Memoriam Christopher Morley," p. 4.
25. Oakley, *Christopher Morley on Long Island*, p. 28.
26. *The Ironing Board*, p. 27.
27. *A Book of Great Autobiography*, p. 15.
28. *Shakespeare and Hawaii*, p. 54.
29. *Streamlines* (Garden City, 1939), p. 48.
30. *Ex Libris Carissimis*, pp. 67 & 116.
31. Oakley, *Christopher Morley on Long Island*, p. 28.

Selected Bibliography

PRIMARY SOURCES

1. Novels and Stories (Chronologically listed)

Parnassus on Wheels. Garden City: Doubleday, Doran & Company, 1917.
The Haunted Bookshop. Garden City: Doubleday, Doran & Company, 1919.
In the Sweet Dry and Dry. (with Bart Haley) New York: Boni and Liveright, 1919.
Kathleen. Garden City: Doubleday, Page & Company, 1920.
Tales from a Rolltop Desk. Garden City: Doubleday Page & Company, 1921.
Where the Blue Begins. Garden City: Doubleday, Page & Company, 1922.
Pandora Lifts the Lid. (with Don Marquis) New York: George H. Doran Company, 1924.
Thunder on the Left. Garden City: Doubleday, Page & Company, 1925.
Pleased to Meet You. Garden City: Doubleday, Page & Company, 1927.
I Know a Secret. Garden City: Doubleday, Page & Company, 1927.
Rudolph and Amina (or The Black Crook). New York: John Day Company, 1930.
John Mistletoe. Garden City: Doubleday, Doran & Company, 1931.
Human Being. Garden City: Doubleday, Doran & Company, 1931.
Swiss Family Manhattan. Doubleday, Doran & Company, 1933.
The Trojan Horse. New York: J. B. Lippincott Co., 1937.
Kitty Foyle. New York: J. B. Lippincott Co., 1939.
Thorofare. New York: Harcourt, Brace and Company, 1942.
The Man Who Made Frinds With Himself. Garden City: Doubleday & Company, 1949.

2. Poetry

The Eighth Sin. London: Blackwell, 1912.
Songs for a Little House. New York: George H. Doran Company, 1917.
The Rocking Horse. New York: George H. Doran Company, 1919.
Hide and Seek. New York: George H. Doran Company, 1920.

133

Chimneysmoke. New York: George H. Doran Company, 1921.
Translations from the Chinese. New York: George H. Doran Company,. 1922.
Parson's Pleasure. New York: George H. Doran Company, 1923.
Translations from the Chinese (enlarged edition). New York: George H. Doran Company, 1927.
Toulemonde. Garden City: Doubleday, Doran & Company, 1928.
Mandarin in Manhattan. Garden City: Doubleday, Doran & Company, 1933.
The Middle Kingdom. New York: Harcourt, Brace and Company, 1944.
Spirit Level and Other Poems. Cambridge: Harvard University Press, 1946.
The Old Mandarin. New York: Harcourt, Brace and Company, 1947.
Poetry Package. (with William Rose Benét) New York: Louis Greenfield, 1950.
The Ballad of New York, New York. Garden City: Doubleday & Company, 1950.
Gentlemen's Relish. New York: Norton, 1955.

3. Essays

Shandygaff. Garden City: Garden City Publishing Co., 1918.
Mince Pie. Garden City: Doubleday, Page & Company, 1919.
Travels in Philadelphia. Philadelphia: McKay, 1920.
Pipefuls. Garden City: Doubleday, Page & Company, 1920.
Plum Pudding. Garden City: Doubleday, Page & Company, 1922.
The Powder of Sympathy. Garden City: Doubleday, Page & Company, 1923.
Inward Ho! Garden City: Doubleday, Page & Company, 1923.
Religio Journalistici. Garden City: Doubleday, Page & Company, 1924.
The Romany Stain. Garden City: Doubleday, Page & Co., 1926.
Off the Deep End. Garden City: Doubleday, Doran & Co., 1928.
Internal Revenue. Garden City: Doubleday, Doran & Co., 1933.
Christopher Morley's Briefcase. Philadelphia: J. B. Lippincott Company, 1936.
Streamlines. Garden City: Doubleday, Doran & Company, 1936.
History of an Autumn. Philadelphia: J. B. Lippincott Company, 1938.
Letters of Askance. New York: J. B. Lippincott Co., 1939.
The Ironing Board. Garden City: Doubleday & Company, 1949.

4. Plays

One-Act Plays. Garden City: Doubleday, Page & Company, 1924.
Really, My Dear. New York: William Edwin Rudge, 1928.
Good Theatre. In Church, Virginia, *Curtain!* New York: Harper & Brothers, 1932.

The Trojan Horse. New York: Random House, 1941.

5. Prefaces and Introductions

Two Prefaces by Walt Whitman. Garden City: Doubleday, Page & Company, 1926.
The Complete Sherlock Holmes. Garden City: Doubleday & Company, 1927.
The Short Stories of Saki. Garden City: Doubleday, Doran & Company, 1930.
The Complete Plays of William Shakespeare. Garden City: Doubleday, Doran & Company, 1936.
Tristram Shandy. Garden City: Doubleday, Doran & Company, 1938.
Leaves of Grass. Garden City: Doubleday, Doran & Company, 1940.
Bacon's Essays. Garden City: Doubleday, Doran & Company, 1944.
The Best of Don Marquis. Garden City: Doubleday & Company, 1946.
Boswell's London Journal. Garden City: Doubleday & Company, 1950.
Prefaces Without Books. (A collection of Morley's Prefaces) Austin: University of Texas Press, 1970.

6. Works Edited

Modern Essays. Garden City: Doubleday, Page & Company, 1921.
Modern Essays, Second Series. New York: Harcourt, Brace and Company, 1924.
The Bowling Green. Garden City: Doubleday, Page & Company, 1924.
A Book of Days. New York, John Day Company, 1930.
Bartlett's Familiar Quotations (Eleventh Edition). Boston: Little, Brown, 1933.
Ex Libris. (Anthology compiled for National Book Fair) New York: Haddon Craftsmen, 1936.
Bartlett's Familiar Quotations (Twelfth Edition). Boston: Little, Brown, 1948.

7. Other Works

Conrad and the Reporters (Joseph Conrad's visit to America). Garden City: Doubleday, Page & Company, 1923.
Hostages to Fortune. Haverford: The Haverfordian, 1925.
The Arrow. Garden City: Doubleday, Page & Company, 1927.
Seacoast of Bohemia. Garden City: Doubleday, Doran & Company, 1929.
Born in a Beer Garden, or She Troupes to Conquer. (with Cleon Throckmorton and Ogden Nash.) New York: The Foundry Press, 1930.
"Eighth Sin." *Colophon Book Collector's Quarterly,* 1930.
Ex Libris Carissimis. Philadelphia: University of Pennsylvania Press, 1932.

Shakespeare and Hawaii. Garden City: Doubleday, Doran & Company, 1933.

Hasta la Vista. (Travel book on Peru.) Garden City: Doubleday, Doran & Company, 1935.

8. Manuscript Materials

The Christopher Morley Collection. The University of Texas. This is the largest collection of Morley materials in existence; it consists of the files of letters that Morley received throughout his lifetime, carbon copies of many of the letters that he sent, the manuscripts of a number of his published works, and other biographical information contained in eleven journals, thirty-two diaries, and one hundred and one memorandum books.

The Christopher Morley Collection. The Haverford College Library. A fairly extensive collection of letters from Morley to various persons, with examples of their correspondence with him.

The Berg Collection. The New York Public Library. Contains several manuscript items of interest, including early notations for *John Mistletoe,* an early autobiography.

SECONDARY SOURCES

ADCOCK, St. JOHN. *The Glory That Was Grub Street.* New York: Frederick A. Stokes Company, 1928. Brief, early sketch of Morley, along with some of his contemporaries.

ALTICK, RICHARD D. "Average Citizen in Grub Street: Christopher Morley After Twenty-five Years," *South Atlantic Quarterly,* XLI (January, 1942), 18 - 31. Thoughtful study; it is unfortunate that Dr. Altick wrote prior to *The Man Who Made Friends With Himself,* however, since that might have answered some of the questions he raised.

ANTHONY, EDWARD. *O Rare Don Marquis.* Garden City: Doubleday & Company, 1962. Includes careful documentation of Morley's close relationship with Marquis, as well as other of their mutual friends.

ATKINSON, J. BROOKS. "Bourgeois Life in an Optimist's Mirror," *Independent,* p. 49. Brief comments about Morley's work.

BENDER, J. TERRY. "Christopher Morley, A Comprehensive Exhibition . . ." Printed by the Castlereagh Press for The Hofstra University Library, 1970. Brochure of the documents assembled for this major exhibit; the descriptions are especially strong in Morley juvenilia and special or pre-publication editions of Morley's works.

BRACKER, JON. "Introduction" to *Bright Cages, Selected Poems and Translations from the Chinese by Christopher Morley.* Philadelphia: University of Pennsylvania Press, 1965. Twenty-one-page biographical sketch and discussion of some aspects of Morley's poetry in depth.

————. "An Exhibition of C[hristopher] D[arlington] M[orley] Manuscripts & First Editions . . . ." Printed for the Humanities Research Center by the Printing Division of The University of Texas. Illustrated brochure identifying items which illustrate Morley's career; extensive quotations from Morley material.

BREIT, HARVEY. "Talk with Christopher Morley," *The New York Times Book Review*, July 31, 1949, p. 13. Brief journalistic interview gives Morley's opinions on subjects other than his own activities.

CANBY, HENRY SEIDEL. *American Estimates*. New York: Harcourt, Brace and Company, 1929. Eight-page sketch of Morley as a co-worker.

"Christopher Morley, His History Done by Divers Hands . . . ." New York: Doubleday, Page & Company, 1922. Morley's hand can be seen in much of this charming and informative seventeen-page publicity brochure; extensive autobiographical quotations from Morley included.

GORDON, MILTON M. "Kitty Foyle and the Concept of Class as Culture," *American Journal of Sociology* (November, 1947), pp. 210 - 17. Interesting, if not entirely convincing, study of *Kitty Foyle* from a different perspective than the usual literary one.

HUGHES, BABETTE. *Christopher Morley, Multi ex Uno*. Seattle: University of Washington, 1927. Short, early study of Morley's many-faceted literary career.

"In Memoriam Christopher Morley." New York: Book-of-the-Month Club, 1957. Ten-page brochure sent to club members following Morley's death; contains articles by Clifton Fadiman, John P. Marquand, Norman Cousins, Harrison Smith, and J. Donald Adams. Marquand's contribution is the least conventional.

KAMMER, A. S. "Wallace Stevens and Christopher Morley," *Furioso 3* (Winter, 1948), pp. 50 - 51. Extended treatment of a relatively minor coincidence.

KUNITZ, STANLEY, J. *Twentieth Century Authors*. New York: H. W. Wilson Company, 1955. Brief sketch of Morley made late in his career.

LEE, ALFRED P. *A Bibliography of Christopher Morley*. New York: Doubleday, Doran & Company, 1935. Contains full collations for books by Morley through *Hasta la Vista*.

LYLE, GUY R. and BROWN, H. TATNALL, JR. *A Bibliography of Christopher Morley*. Washington: The Scarecrow Press, 1952. Contains only title entries for books through *Hasta la Vista*, with full collations for all later works published by 1952.

LYLE, GUY R. "Ethos of a Man of Letters," *Emory University Quarterly* (Fall, 1963), pp. 137 - 43. Largely an enthusiastic review of Morley's last novel.

McCORD, DAVID. "Christopher Morley," *English Journal* (January, 1930), pp. 1 - 9. Pleasant, brief sketch by an admirer.

MATTHEWS, T. S. "Christopher Morley," *New Republic*, March 21, 1928, pp. 167 - 69. Perhaps overly brief sketch.

MORLEY, FRANK V. "Christopher Morley, or The Treasure of the Abandoned
    Mine." Unpublished photostatic copy of text of a talk given at Haver-
    ford College, October 19, 1958, together with his introductory
    remarks. In the University of Texas Collection. It is intimately infor-
    mative about Christopher Morley, perceptive, and charmingly written
    by Morley's brother.
————. *My One Contribution to Chess.* New York: Huebsch, 1945. This
    deceptively titled, 113-page volume is more about Frank Morley's
    way of playing chess — and living — than about the game itself;
    numerous references to Christopher are present, as well as some
    remarks by him. Readable and highly recommended.
OAKLEY, HELEN McK. *Christopher Morley on Long Island.* Roslyn: The
    Christopher Morley Knothole Association, 1967. Lovely, well-
    illustrated booklet of twenty-eight pages; written for the opening of
    Christopher Morley Park on Long Island, it emphasizes Morley's con-
    tacts with the Long Island region.
O'SULLIVAN, VINCENT. "America and the English Literary Tradition," *Liv-
    ing Age,* October 18, 1919, pp. 170 - 76. Discussion of Morley's early
    poetry and essays respecting various English writers.
OVERTON, GRANT. *American Nights Entertainment.* New York: Appleton,
    1923. Contains a sixteen-page article, "The Unclassified Case of
    Christopher Morley," which is speculative, but refreshing in its ap-
    proach to Morley's early work.
RIESENBERG, FELIX. *Living Again, an Autobiography.* New York: Double-
    day, Doran and Company, 1939. Fifteen pages are devoted to this
    close friend's reminiscences of Morley.
VAN DOREN, CARL. "Day In and Day Out: Adams, Morley, Marquis, and
    Broun, Manhattan Wits," *Century* (December, 1923), pp. 308 - 15.
    Interesting from the social, rather than the literary point of view.
VAN GELDER, ROBERT. *Writers and Writing.* New York: Scribner's Sons,
    1946. Three-page interview which ran originally in the *New York
    Herald Tribune;* journalistic, but contains some interesting informa-
    tion.
WALLACH, MARK I. "Escaped Into Print: A Study of Christopher Morley."
    Unpublished honors thesis examining Morley's own view of himself
    and his work; available from the Christopher Morley Knothole
    Association, or in the Wesleyan University Honors College Library.
————. "The Columns and Essays of Christopher Morley," *The Markham
    Review* (February, 1972), pp. 33 - 37. Revised version of portion of
    "Escaped Into Print," *supra.*
WARFEL, HARRY R. *American Novelists of Today.* New York: American
    Book Company, 1951. Short study late in Morley's career; some useful
    information.

WILLIAMS, W. L. G. "Christopher Morley as I Remember Him," *American Oxonian* (July, 1957), pp. 158 - 63. Informative, charmingly written memoir by a close friend of Morley's; contains none of the conventional phrases usually found in obituaries.

Index